Hallaj

Hallaj

Poems of a Sufi Martyr

Husayn ibn Mansur al-Hallaj

Translated from the Arabic by Carl W. Ernst

NORTHWESTERN UNIVERSITY PRESS

EVANSTON, ILLINOIS

Northwestern University Press
www.nupress.northwestern.edu

Support for this publication came in part through the Global Humanities Initiative,
which is jointly supported by Northwestern University's Buffett Institute for
Global Studies and the Alice Kaplan Institute for the Humanities.

Printed in the United States of America

10   9   8   7   6   5   4   3   2   1

Library of Congress Cataloging-in-Publication Data

Names: Ḥallāj, al-Ḥusayn ibn Manṣūr, 858 or 859–922, author. | Ernst, Carl W., 1950–
   translator.
Title: Hallaj : poems of a Sufi martyr / Husayn ibn Mansur al-Hallaj ; translated from
   the Arabic by Carl W. Ernst.
Description: Evanston, Illinois : Northwestern University Press, 2018. | Includes
   bibliographical references and indexes.
Identifiers: LCCN 2018001226 | ISBN 9780810137356 (pbk. : alk. paper) | ISBN
   9780810137363 (ebook)
Subjects: LCSH: Hallaj, al-Husayn ibn Mansur, 858 or 859–922—Translations into
   English. | Sufi poetry, Arabic—Early works to 1800.
Classification: LCC PJ7745.H3 A2 2018 | DDC 892.7134—dc23

LC record available at https://lccn.loc.gov/2018001226

Coniugi dilectissimae

CONTENTS

VIII. Union

PREFACE AND ACKNOWLEDGMENTS

I first encountered the poems of Hallaj in a graduate seminar with the late Professor Annemarie Schimmel at Harvard many years ago. A number of these captivating verses also appeared in my dissertation, published in 1983 as *Words of Ecstasy in Sufism*. I eventually decided to take on the challenge of translating a comprehensive selection of these poems, after having inflicted them on my own graduate students for a number of years—most memorably in a 2009 seminar on Hallaj attended by several intrepid souls (Rose Aslan, Tehseen Thaver, Kevin Blankenship, and Recep Alpyagil), and more recently with Micah Hughes, Dr. Rodrigo Adem, and Jay Yeo. I would like to express my thanks to all of these "Hallajians" for joining me in the close reading of these texts. I have received encouragement and valuable suggestions from many colleagues, including Abdul Sattar Jawad, Mbaye Lo, miriam cooke, Bruce Lawrence, Nasrollah Pourjavady, Arin Salamah Qudsi, Muhsin Musawi, Th. Emil Homerin, Peter Burian, Maura High, Stefan Sperl, Ahmed Moustafa, and Nelly van Doorn. Many thanks to them all.

I would also like to acknowledge with thanks the significant support this project has received through a 2010 research fellowship from the Medieval and Early Modern Studies Program at the University of North Carolina at Chapel Hill, and a 2010 fellowship from the John Simon Guggenheim Memorial Foundation (the first year for awards in the category of translation). Thanks are also due to the William R. Kenan, Jr. Charitable Trust for ongoing support of my research. In addition, I would like to express my gratitude to the Buffett Institute for Global Studies at Northwestern University for the award of the Global Humanities Translation Prize in 2017. Most of all, I want to express my profound gratitude to my wife Judy Ernst, without whom none of this would have been possible; this work is dedicated to her.

Introduction

Prologue: A Hidden Book

In the eastern Iranian city of Nishapur, a little over a thousand years ago, a young Sufi named al-Qushayri was sent by his father-in-law and teacher, al-Daqqaq (d. 1016), to steal a book. This book was in the library of al-Daqqaq's own teacher, the venerable al-Sulami (937–1021), who perhaps more than anyone else in Khurasan defined the shape of early Islamic mysticism. Al-Qushayri (986–1074), who himself became a celebrated early authority on Sufism, relates this story in the following words:

> One day I was with Abu `Ali al-Hasan ibn `Ali al-Daqqaq, and the tale was told of Abu `Abd Allah al-Sulami that he would stand up at a musical performance in harmony with the Sufis [i.e., in ecstasy]. Abu `Ali said, "For someone in a spiritual state like his, it is perhaps better to be quiet about him." Then he said to me, "Go to him; you will find him standing in his library. In front of the books is a small red square booklet, in which are the poems of al-Husayn ibn Mansur [al-Hallaj]. Get that booklet, and don't tell him anything, but bring it to me." And this was at midday.
>
> So I went to Abu `Abd al-Rahman [al-Sulami], who was in his library, and the booklet was located as was mentioned. . . . I was completely bewildered and asked myself: "How should I behave in this situation between those two?" I mulled over this matter in my thoughts and decided: "There's nothing left for me but truth!" So I said, "The Master Abu `Ali [al-Daqqaq] described this booklet, and told me, 'Bring it to me without asking the master's permission,' but I am afraid, and I cannot disobey him; what is your command?"
>
> Then he brought out another collection of the sayings of al-Husayn ibn Mansur, in which is one of his writings, called *The Cabinet on the Destruction of Eras*. He said, "Take this, and tell him, 'I have read this booklet, and I transmit verses from it in my writings.'" So I left.[1]

Qushayri, who would go on to become a major figure in early Sufism, must have been a novice at the time of this episode (in 1006 he would have been twenty years old, and Daqqaq must have been over forty, while Sulami would have been seventy-one). He would have been in an extremely awkward position; his master Daqqaq had made a disparaging remark about Daqqaq's own teacher, the formidable Sulami, implying that the latter was overly prone to go into ecstasy at musical performances. Then Daqqaq basically told Qushayri to steal a book from Sulami's library, which had to be extensive; Sulami was the first major author to synthesize the teachings of Sufism. When Qushayri was detected and confessed his dilemma to the senior shaykh, Sulami fobbed him off with an obscure work by Hallaj on the cycles of time and instructed him to relate that he had read Hallaj's poems and was quoting them.[2] This story draws attention to the poetry of Hallaj as a controversial item even among Sufis; its aura of mystery is heightened by placing it in the context of debates about yielding to ecstasy at a concert of Sufi music.

This curious story has been widely told—not only in Qushayri's own *Epistle on Sufism* but also in the *History of Baghdad* by al-Khatib al-Baghdadi and in other scholarly works. Yet Qushayri failed to obey the commands of either of his Sufi masters. He did not procure the small red volume of poems of Hallaj for Daqqaq, and while he may have conveyed the other book to Daqqaq as Sulami ordered, his account draws attention to the fact that he himself did not in fact transmit the poems of Hallaj in his own writings. Although Qushayri quoted the extensive theological creed of Hallaj and mentioned him a few times in passing in his *Epistle*, he decided not to honor Hallaj with a biography alongside the other founding figures of Sufism. While not as circumspect as Abu Bakr Kalabadhi (d. 990), another Sufi authority who referred to Hallaj only obliquely, as "one of the great ones," Qushayri evidently concluded that the poetry of Hallaj, like the ecstasy of Sulami, was best not spoken of.[3] The fact that he publicly recorded this episode nevertheless underlines Qushayri's implicit recognition of the poems of Hallaj as important texts, which nevertheless should not be discussed in public.

A few years after that incident in Nishapur, `Ali al-Hujwiri (d. ca. 1073), another early Sufi author, recorded the details of his own uncanny encounter with Hallaj's poetry in a Sufi retreat in Palestine:

> Once I set out from Damascus with two dervishes to visit Ibn al-Mu`alla, who was living in the country near Ramla. On the way we arranged that each of us should think of the matter concerning which we were in doubt, in order that that venerable director might tell us our secret thoughts and solve our difficulties. I said to myself: "I will desire of him the poems and intimate supplications (*munajat*) of Husayn b.

Mansur (al-Hallaj)." One of my companions said, "I will desire him to pray that my disease of the spleen (*tihal*) may become better"; and the other said, "I will wish for sweetmeat of different colours" (*halwa-yi sabuni*). As soon as we arrived, Ibn al-Mu`alla commanded that a manuscript of the poems and supplications of Husayn should be presented to me, and laid his hand on the belly of the invalid so that his illness was assuaged, and said to the other dervish: "Parti-coloured sweetmeat is eaten by soldiers (`awanan*); you are dressed as a saint, and the dress of a saint does not accord with the appetite of a soldier. Choose one or the other."[4]

Unlike Qushayri (whose works he was also familiar with), Hujwiri obtained his copy of the poems and prayers of Hallaj just for the asking. It is nevertheless striking that in both cases the hidden desires of Qushayri and Hujwiri were transparent to the Sufi masters they were visiting, as would be expected in the milieu of Islamic mysticism. The outcomes differed, however; unlike Qushayri, Hujwiri decided to include a biography of Hallaj among those of the other early masters in his Persian treatise on Sufism, *Revelation of the Mystery* (*Kashf al-mahjub*).[5] This brief account of Hallaj was friendly, though it contained critical remarks about his spiritual immaturity. Hujwiri also indicated that he wrote two separate books on Hallaj, one a commentary on his sayings and the other an account of his life (unfortunately, neither work survives). Adding to the complexity of the situation, Hujwiri remarked on the "heretics who pretend to be the followers of al-Hallaj and make his sayings an argument for their heresy," and he included a chapter on these "Hallajiyya" as one of two Sufi-based heretical groups whose teachings were incompatible with Islam.[6]

From the deeply ambiguous treatment of Hallaj in the anecdotes related by Qushayri and Hujwiri, two major points emerge. One is that even the admirers of Hallaj felt compelled to mute or conceal their enthusiasm, due to the controversy attached to his name and writings. The other conclusion that may be drawn is that there was considerable interest focused on the collected poems and prayers of Hallaj, even if they were unavailable. What were these poems, and how were they interpreted? These are the questions that animate this book.

The Legend of Hallaj

On March 26, 922, the city of Baghdad witnessed the end of a tragedy. On that day, officials of the `Abbasid caliphate supervised the public execution of al-Husayn ibn Mansur al-Hallaj, a wayward Sufi mystic. His execution was the culmination of a series of heresy trials involving Hallaj and his associates, a legal process that had lasted over a decade. The tale itself has often been told, in different ways, and it would be tempting here to offer a summary or a digest, leaving aside the miracle stories as is customary for historians today. One could present in this way a plausible narrative with some claim to historical accuracy.[7]

This indeed was the approach of Louis Massignon in his lifelong study of the career of Hallaj, which will be discussed in more detail below. Massignon began his massive *Passion of Hallaj* with translations of the oldest surviving biographical accounts of Hallaj, as far as he could reconstruct them. These primitive texts include a brief portrait of Hallaj by the Sufi scholar Qannad (d. 941) and a more extensive version as related by Hallaj's son Hamd.[8] Correlating this information with other sources, such as the thirty-page biography of Hallaj in the great *History of Baghdad* by al-Khatib al-Baghdadi (d. 1071), Massignon attempted to create a year-by-year narrative of the details of the life and death of Hallaj and the aftermath.[9] The story is complex and full of contradictions.

Hallaj was denounced as a sorcerer and praised as a saint. He was accused of claiming to be the incarnation of God or possibly the Messiah, and he was also charged with being an agent of the Shi`i revolutionary movement of the Qarmatis. He was imprisoned off and on and subjected to interrogations by viziers and their legal advisers. His trials took place at a time when the `Abbasid Empire was experiencing a crisis of major proportions and the government was in serious financial, political, and military disarray. The final trial, dominated by political factionalism and questionable procedures, condemned Hallaj as an apostate on a technicality; the last straw was his reported opinion that those lacking the means to undertake the hajj, the pilgrimage to Mecca, could create a symbolic Ka`ba in their homes, which would fulfill this religious duty.[10]

Despite this condemnation of him, subsequent literature reveals that Hallaj continued to draw reactions both positive and negative, but few major figures could avoid addressing the questions he raised. Hallaj's martyrdom seems to have been much on the mind of several later figures who shared his fate, such as the Persian Sufi `Ayn al-Qudat al-Hamadani (d. 1132) and the Illuminationist philosopher Shihab al-Din al-Suhrawardi (d. 1191), both of whom were executed for their radical views. His champions include such notable figures as Abu Hamid al-Ghazali (d. 1111) and Jalal al-Din Rumi (d. 1273). Ghazali's judgment on the correctness of Hallaj's spiritual state was tempered, however, by his declaration that revealing that secret was a crime punishable by death.[11]

The legend of Hallaj has obscured both his life and his death. Perhaps the most compelling portrait of Hallaj by a later author is the biography that Farid al-Din `Attar placed at the end of his *Memoir of the Saints*. There, we are told, the real reason for Hallaj's execution was his public utterance of the daring statement "I am the Truth" (*ana al-haqq*), a brazen claim to divinity that was seen as utter heresy. Indeed, `Attar provides the gripping detail that the death verdict was delivered by Hallaj's own teacher, the respected Sufi master Junayd, who nevertheless had to remove his Sufi garb and don the costume of a judge before he gave the judicial decree (*fatwa*); `Attar's powerful narrative is marred here by the contradictory fact that Junayd had actually died twelve years before the execution of Hallaj. `Attar nevertheless goes on to relate the truly miraculous end of Hallaj, who continues to cry, "I am the Truth," after his head is struck off. And even after his body is burned, the ashes call out the same declaration as they are scattered in the Tigris. This dramatic account by `Attar has tended to frame the interpretation of Hallaj's fate for subsequent Sufi-minded readers, who have seen this story as a collision between mysticism and the law.[12]

Hallaj is often portrayed as a central figure of Sufism, the tradition of spiritual and ethical practice that was beginning to take shape in his time, though its full contours as a social and religious trend would take centuries to unfold.[13] Moreover, Hallaj's relationship to the central figures of Baghdadian Sufism (such as Junayd, Sahl al-Tustari, and `Amr al-Makki) was conflicted; stories are told of his disagreements with them, sometimes including prophecies of his untimely end. One of the key differences between Hallaj and the emerging Sufi establishment was that the latter emphasized teaching only the spiritual elite. A Sufi technical language was formed to communicate esoteric ideas. Hallaj mastered this discipline but felt compelled to reveal his experiences to a wider public. Narratives preserved in *News of Hallaj* (see appendix 3) depict Hallaj on the streets of Baghdad proclaiming to the people his tortured relationship with God in scenes of surprising emotional intensity.

Hallaj's ambivalent relationship with the Sufis is summarized as follows by al-Khatib al-Baghdadi:

> He was born in Wasit, or, it is said, Tustar, and went to Baghdad to mix with the Sufis, and was in the company of their masters Junayd ibn Muhammad, Abu al-Husayn al-Nuri, and `Amr al-Makki. But the Sufis disagree about him. Most of them denied that he was one of them, declining to count him among them, but some of their leaders accepted him, such as Abu al-`Abbas ibn `Ata' al-Baghdadi, Muhammad

ibn Khafif al-Shirazi, and Ibrahim ibn Muhammad al-Nasrabadi al-Nisaburi. They considered his spiritual state to be correct, and they collected his sayings; Ibn Khafif said, "al-Husayn ibn Mansur is a divine master [`alim rabbani`]." Those who rejected him accused him of sleight of hand in his activity, and heresy in his belief, but till today he has followers who are connected to him and who adore him.[14]

Ruzbihan al-Baqli, the devoted commentator on Hallaj, gave a more impassioned and more admiring account in his Arabic compendium of the ecstatic sayings of the Sufis, the *Mantiq al-asrar*:

There is one among them who was killed by his claim, and consumed by its meaning; the phoenix of Mt. Qaf of pre-eternity, the sun of the dawnings of the longings of power, the destroyer of the elemental dungeon, the swimmer in the ocean of eternity, Abu al-Mughith Husayn ibn Mansur al-Hallaj. He stood by himself between highest truth and lowest lie. People were astounded at his station; among the subjects of this tale, he was between acceptance and rejection, but in their view he was closer to rejection.

This is the last of the ecstatic speakers whose names I have collected with descriptions of their states. My final goal in writing this book is the explanation of the ecstatic expressions of Hallaj and the clarification of his deeds and words. Love for him impelled me to comment on his speech in ecstatic sayings, and his allusion to selfhood for his lovers and his enemies, for one of the wonderful things about his station was that people were amazed at the aims of his speech, not knowing the subtleties of his allusions. Some denied him, some rejected him, some approved, and some realized his path. So I began the commentary on his sayings to unveil the cloud of doubts from the crescent moon of his pure states for the insight of the faithful with the hints of the masters. Then I added to his words the ecstatic sayings of some of the masters, from my love of them, so it would be an adequate book for those illuminated by the lights of their secret proofs and their deeds in ecstasy and raptures.

For Husayn ibn Mansur fell into the sea of pre-eternity and post-eternity; he entered it with the character of a servant, and he departed it in the garb of lordship. From his deeds and words appeared what is unsuitable to the understanding of the people. Some said he was a sorcerer, some said he was a madman, some said he was deluded, and some said he was a heretic; a few among them said he was truthful. For this is the custom of God, which befell the prophets and messengers, as God said: "The people rejected Noah" (Qur'an 27.105), Abraham, Moses, Jethro, Salih, Jesus, John, Zacharia, and Muhammad. God most high said about the Meccan infidels' saying about his Prophet's truth: "They say he is possessed" (Qur'an 68:51), "this is a lying sorcerer" (Qur'an 38.4). They accused him of poetry, sorcery, quackery, and madness. So God most high rejected them by saying, "Those to whom we revealed the book know him just as they know their sons, but a group among them are concealing the truth" (Qur'an 2:146). You should understand that the people of Baghdad observed the miracles of Husayn during his execution, before his execution, after his execution, and during his imprisonment. They saw the truthfulness of his claim and the realities of his words in his writings inscribed with clear proofs.

They knew he was "a divine master," but the scholars and the political elite envied him and accused him of infidelity, seeking to increase their power. But God was aware of their scheming, and he does not guide schemers. Our master and lord Abu `Abd Allah Muhammad ibn Khafif, Abu al-`Abbas ibn `Ata', Shibli, and Abu al-Qasim al-Nasrabadi bore witness to his truthfulness; they accepted him and approved of his state and his allusion, so that Shaykh Abu `Abd Allah said, "Husayn ibn Mansur is a divine master." This was said in Baghdad; he recited his virtues and related his miracles at Bab al-Taq. And I have heard that Abu al-`Abbas ibn Surayj did not approve his execution and gave no decree for the shedding of his blood.

Husayn was eloquent regarding mystical knowledge, the divine unity, "the isolation of the eternal from the temporal." I have heard that he composed a thousand books on all subjects, which his enviers burned after his execution. He has sweet poetry, noble words, manifest miracles, and writings on all topics—may God bless him in his life and death, and God's mercy to his brothers among the people of this tale and his lovers in their suffering, until the day of Resurrection![15]

These testimonies are examples of the remarkable impact of Hallaj, but even his admirers had to acknowledge the ambiguity of his reception.

The Writings of Hallaj

A major dilemma confronts anyone interested in the writings of Hallaj. He was, by all accounts, a prolific author, but very little of his work has survived; indeed, it is widely believed that his writings were deliberately suppressed. Ruzbihan Baqli remarks that, according to the traditions of the

Sufis of Fars, Hallaj had written a thousand books and "they burned most of them in Baghdad."[16] While that number may be an exaggeration, the tenth-century bibliographer Abu al-Faraj Muhammad al-Warraq al-Nadim (d. 990), in his comprehensive listing of all known writings in Arabic that is known as *The Index* (*al-Fihrist*), records the titles of forty-six works by Hallaj on a surprising variety of topics, ranging from metaphysics to politics (see appendix 2).[17] Hujwiri said he had seen fifty works by Hallaj in Iraq and Persia, calling him "the author of brilliant compositions and allegories and polished sayings in theology and jurisprudence."[18] Almost none of this survives. What remains of the literary production of Hallaj (all in Arabic) can be classified into four categories: (1) mystical sayings (including comments on Qur'anic verses, amounting to around 350 quotations);[19] (2) the *Riwayat*, twenty-seven hadith-like sayings that are related not by human beings but by cosmic entities;[20] (3) a series of essays on mystical topics entitled *Kitab al-Tawasin*, also preserved in a Persian translation and commentary by Ruzbihan;[21] and (4) his collected poems, which by convention of Arabic literature are now called the *Diwan al-Hallaj*.

The existing collection of poems attributed to Hallaj is largely the result of Louis Massignon's efforts, although subsequent editors such as Kamil Mustafa al-Shaybi have corrected and improved on Massignon's pioneering work (see appendix 4).[22] But as we have seen, traces of this collection have existed previously, including the "small red square booklet" containing the poems of Hallaj, preserved in the library of the eminent Sufi scholar of Nishapur, al-Sulami; it must have been considered both rare and controversial. Likewise Hujwiri's report testifies to the circulation of the "poems and intimate supplications" of Hallaj in Palestine.[23] These reports on a body of poetry by Hallaj confirm the widely repeated comment of al-Khatib al-Baghdadi, the historian of Baghdad, that "al-Hallaj had a beauty of expression and a sweetness of language, and poetry according to the path [*tariqa*] of Sufism."[24] Still, it appears that there was no *Diwan* or "collected poems" of Hallaj to parallel the collected poetry of the major figures of Arabic literature; instead, it seems that the poems of Hallaj were always embedded in mixed works alongside prayers and stories about Hallaj. It would be left to Massignon to create the *Diwan al-Hallaj* for the first time in his critical edition of 1931 (see appendix 4).

Some of the longer fragments by Hallaj that have survived in early Sufi works testify to his great impact on the formation of Sufi doctrine. For instance, one text of fundamental importance is Hallaj's creed, or declaration of faith, on the unity of God, which was introduced (with minor variations) in the opening pages of two of the fundamental early syntheses of Sufism, the *Book Introducing the Teaching of the Sufis* by Kalabadhi (d. 990) and the

Epistle on Sufism by Qushayri (completed in 1045). Here is Kalabadhi's text (quoting Hallaj anonymously), which provides the flavor of Hallaj's characteristic use of ordinary language to describe the transcendence of God:

> One of the great Sufis said in a discourse of his: " 'Before' does not outstrip Him, 'after' does not interrupt Him, 'of' does not vie with Him for precedence, 'from' does not accord with Him, 'to' does not join with Him, 'in' does not inhabit Him, 'when' does not stop Him, 'if' does not consult with Him, 'over' does not overshadow Him, 'under' does not support Him, 'opposite' does not face Him, 'with' does not press Him, 'behind' does not take hold of Him, 'before' does not limit Him, 'previous' does not display Him, 'after' does not cause Him to pass away, 'all' does not unite Him, 'is' does not bring Him to being, 'is not' does not deprive Him of being. Concealment does not veil Him. His pre-existence preceded time, His being preceded not-being, His eternity preceded limit. If you say 'when', His existing has outstripped time; if you say 'before', before is after Him; if you say 'he', 'h' and 'e' are His creation; if you say 'how', His essence is veiled from description; if you say 'where', His being preceded space; if you say 'ipseity' (*ma huwa*), His ipseity (*huwiyah*) is apart from things. Other than He cannot be qualified by two (opposite) dualities at one time; and yet with Him they do not create opposition. He is hidden in His manifestation, manifest in His concealing. He is outward and inward, near and far; and in this respect He is removed beyond the resemblance of creation. He acts without contact, instructs without meeting, guides without pointing. Desires do not conflict with Him, thoughts do not mingle with Him: His essence is without qualification (*takyif*), His action without effort (*taklif*)."[25]

This densely written passage demonstrates key characteristics of Hallaj's style—antithesis, breaking down language into prepositional units, and paradox—that also characterized the emergence of a specialized technical language for Sufism, as we shall see below.

Another major fragment by Hallaj is a lengthy metaphysical meditation on love as the essence of God, contained in the comprehensive early Arabic treatise on love by Abu al-Hasan al-Daylami, a native of Shiraz who also wrote an important biography of the prominent early Sufi Ibn al-Khafif. In *The Book of the Inclination of the Affectionate Alif towards the Inclined Lam*, Daylami offers a panoramic survey of all the theories of love that had flourished in Arabic literature during the tenth century. This is also a text whose very title, including the wordplay with the names of Arabic letters, is based on a verse by Hallaj (poem 70, "Love Is in Primordial Eternity").[26] It is striking that Daylami felt that Hallaj's views on love were close to the opinions of the ancient Greek philosophers.[27] In any case, the powerful use of the elements of language in Hallaj's teaching on divine unity indicates his cerebral and explosive use of language in poetry.

There is one additional resource to be considered, a collection of dramatic narratives presented as the oral accounts of Hallaj by his close associates, known under the title *News of Hallaj* (*Akhbar al-Hallaj*). This compilation, which contains frequent references to and predictions of Hallaj's execution, was clearly put together by followers of Hallaj, and it probably is similar to the texts described by Qushayri and Hujwiri—it is not a *diwan*, or formal collection of poems, arranged alphabetically by end rhyme but a body of stories containing the "prayers and poems" of Hallaj in vividly conveyed accounts. As a supplement to this book's independent translations of 117 of Hallaj's poems, translations of twenty-two of these narratives are presented in appendix 3, providing the reader with the opportunity to see the full context in which some of Hallaj's verses were transmitted, which admittedly is a different experience than considering each poem as a self-contained text.

The Question of Sufi Poetry

The writings of Hallaj, then, pose a series of problems. A lost archive cannot be evaluated, to be sure. And the modern "reconstruction" of Hallaj's poems (as Massignon labeled his 1931 edition of the *Diwan al-Hallaj*) raises questions about the literary character of the poems attributed to Hallaj. Because of Hallaj's association with the early Sufi movement, can his poetry be called "Sufi poetry"? The diversity of subjects, styles, and imagery in the poems translated here do not demonstrate the kind of generic uniformity that a label like "Sufi poetry" suggests. From a purely formal perspective, some of the poems of Hallaj, if considered on their own terms, would normally fall into such categories as "love poetry," "sermons," and "riddles." In what sense should one understand al-Baghdadi's remark that Hallaj wrote "poetry according to the path of Sufism"?

The early Sufi movement arose in the society of the `Abbasid Empire, an environment that by the late ninth century was saturated with the culture of Arabic literature. Poetry had been enormously important for the pre-Islamic Arabs and continued to serve as a powerful means of communication both in the heartland of the caliphate and in far-flung provinces from North Africa to central Asia. It is not surprising to find that the mystics resorted to the dense literary medium of poetry to convey both deep emotion and abstract insight. Poetry became a natural ancillary to the exposition of Sufi thought on the soul and its experiences and was pervasive in Sufi discourse. Many examples of the power of poetry in Sufi circles are provided in the classic compendium of Sufi practice by Abu Nasr al-Sarraj (d. 988), *The Book of Glimmerings on Sufism* (*Kitab al-luma` fil-tasawwuf*). As Sarraj related,

> I heard al-Wajihi say, I heard al-Tayalasi al-Razi say, I visited Israfil, the teacher of Dhu al-Nun (may God have mercy on them both), and he was sitting and drumming his fingers on the ground, chanting something to himself. When he saw me, he said, "Can you recite something beautiful?" I said, "No." He replied, "You have no heart."[28]

Arabic verses are sprinkled liberally throughout the collections of Sufi teachings that emerged in the late tenth century. In addition to the works of Sulami, Sarraj, and Kalabadhi, other significant sources for such poetry include *The Purification of Consciences* by Abu Sa`d al-Khargushi and *The White and the Black* of Abu al-Hasan al-Sirjani, as we shall see below. The Baghdadian Sufi Ja`far al-Khuldi claimed that he knew by heart the collected poems of 130 Sufis.[29] Many of the verses quoted in early Sufi writings, when they are not anonymous, are credited to the famous pioneers of Baghdadian Sufism, including Junayd, Abu `Ali al-Rudhbari, Sari al-Saqati, Abu al-Husayn al-Nuri, Sumnun al-Muhibb, and others. Surprisingly, this body of Arabic mystical poetry has not received very much scholarly attention.

One of the problems in the study of early Sufi poetry is related to a widespread tendency to identify this mystical tradition primarily with its Iranian and Indian examples, which have been held in contrast to the supposedly inferior spiritual and intellectual capacities of the Semitic races, particularly the Arabs. This prejudice revealed itself from the very beginning of Orientalist scholarship when Sir William Jones delivered an influential lecture to the Asiatic Society of Bengal entitled "On the Mystical Poetry of the Persians and Hindus."[30] This attitude was an example of the larger prejudice against Arabic poetry, which many Orientalist scholars considered to be extravagant and lacking in literary merit.[31]

In more recent years, this opinion could be charitably interpreted as a result of the new and widespread popularity of the Persian poetry of Rumi, who tends to eclipse other figures in Sufi tradition. Indeed, a quick glance at many online booksellers' websites reveals that the category of "Sufi poetry" is mostly limited to freewheeling renderings of the Persian poems of Rumi (and, to a lesser extent, Hafiz), sometimes in postmodern presentations that appear unrelated to any identifiable original text. From this perspective, "Sufi poetry" has become a marketing category in the brisk business of New Age spirituality.

Still, it is remarkable to see how easily an Orientalist scholar like R. A. Nicholson could fall into racial language in his description of Sufi poetry in 1921:

> One of the deepest differences between Arabs and Persians shows itself in the extent and character of the mystical poetry of each people. As regards Persia, the names of Sana'i, `Attar, Jalalu'ddin Rumi, Sa`di, Hafiz, and Jami are witnesses enough. Whether quantity or quality be considered, the best part of medieval Persian poetry is either genuinely mystical in spirit or is so saturated with mystical ideas that it will never be more than half understood by those who read it literally. When we turn to Arabic poetry of the period subsequent to the rise and development of Sufism, what do we find? No lack of poets, certainly, though few of them reach the first rank and their output is scanty compared with the opulent genius of their Persian contemporaries. But from Mutanabbi and Ma`arri down to the bards unknown in Europe who flourished long after the Baghdad Caliphate had fallen, it is remarkable how seldom they possess the note (as Newman would say) of mysticism. The main reason, I think, lies in racial endowment. The Arab has no such passion for an ultimate principle of unity as has always distinguished the Persians and Indians.[32]

Although it may be surprising to some, this kind of racial interpretation of mysticism has proven to be remarkably tenacious. Without going into the details of this problem, it suffices to say that this biased attitude reveals a lack of attention to the phenomenon of Arabic Sufi poetry as a formative component of the Sufi tradition. Ironically, Rumi himself was a great admirer of Arabic poetry, and he regularly adorned his own poems with lines from Hallaj (see appendix 5, "How Rumi Quoted Hallaj").

Defining Sufi poetry is not easy to do, however, and despite the massive presence of poetry in Sufi circles, there is surprisingly little discussion of this question in modern studies of Sufism. A few reflections on this literary phenomenon are therefore necessary. Can one speak of Sufi poetry as a separate genre of poetry, or do various kinds of poetry appear in Sufi writings? My observation is that early Arabic poetry does not have a distinctive category of Sufi poetry. Sufis were fond of different types of poetry, including poems devoted to love, wine, and asceticism, and they had a notable tendency to appropriate selected verses of established poets, often giving them a mystical turn by employing a slight shift in vocabulary.

In formal terms, three types of early Arabic verse helped set the stage for Sufi poetry, as it were. A tradition of ascetic poems (*zuhdiyya*) associated particularly with the eminent poet Abu al-Atahiyya (d. 829) served as one such precedent. This category of poetry is characterized by a moralizing stance criticizing the enticements of the world and was probably seen as a counterbalance to the secular poetry about love and wine that was so dominant in the courtly culture of the early caliphate.[33] This kind of preaching against the attractions of worldly life is indeed a frequent theme in Sufi poetry.

A second model appreciated by Sufi poets was found in the romantic genre of Arabic poetry that emphasized chaste love, a characteristic supposedly found among the Arab tribe of the Banu `Udhra, legendary for their Platonic love affairs; this `Udhri tendency was exemplified by figures like the legendary Majnun, who languished in hopeless longing for his beloved Layla.[34] `Udhri verse also provided a "courtly" model of poetry that stressed the sufferings of the lover, frequently in highly exaggerated yet memorable terms.[35]

A third model is sometimes not acknowledged: the poetry popular among Sufis also drew, undeniably, from the poetry of frankly erotic love and intoxication typified by the great Abu Nuwas (d. ca. 815), the drinking companion of the Caliph al-Amin and a founding figure of the "modernism" of the `Abbasid era.[36] Hujwiri, the early Sufi writer, finds himself quoting a scandalous line from Abu Nuwas—though anonymously—when arguing that listening to poetry and music requires being fully present for God:

> How excellent, though on a frivolous topic, are the words of the poet [Abu Nuwas] who declared his love for wine!
>
> > "Give me wine to drink and tell me it is wine.
> > Do not give it me in secret, when it can be given openly,"
>
> i.e., let my eyes see it and my hand touch it and my palate taste it and my nose smell it: there yet remains one sense to be gratified, viz. my hearing: tell me, therefore, this is wine, that my ear may feel the same delight as my other senses.[37]

Likewise, Ruzbihan Baqli cites the same verse but only attributes it to "one of the lovers."[38] Qushayri, when discussing spiritual intoxication and sobriety, also quotes a verse by Abu Nuwas, but he attributes it to his Sufi teacher and substitutes a Sufi term for intoxication.[39] Thus there are a number of different emphases and twists on preexisting poems to be found in early Arabic Sufi writings.

There are some indications that early Sufi writers were defensive about the attractions of poetry, particularly insofar as the melodious singing of such verses might compete with the recitation of the Qur'an. Therefore one way of justifying the religious value of poetry was to appeal to the example of the Prophet Muhammad. Sarraj observes that Ka'b ibn Zuhayr recited his celebrated ode "Banat Su'ad" in the presence of the Prophet.[40] Likewise, Khargushi records a hadith in which the Prophet praised the pre-Islamic poet Labid as the best of the Arab poets.[41] Despite this nod to the classical Arabic tradition, however, it was uncommon for early Sufis to refer to the corpus of pre-Islamic Arabic poetry (exceptionally, Ibn 'Arabi would later write poems in the ancient Bedouin style).[42] The literary style of most Sufi poetry has much more in common with the contemporary poems of the 'Abbasid era. This connection becomes explicit in a case such as that of the Sufi poet Qannad, who is said to have studied the *diwan* of the famous Abu Tammam (d. 845).[43] Even Qushayri, who does not include much poetry in his writings, quotes verses from the 'Abbasid poet (and one-day caliph) Ibn al-Mu'tazz.[44]

In what still remains the most substantial essay published in English on the nature of Arabic mystical poetry, Annemarie Schimmel briefly outlines three major types of Sufi poems defined by their formal characteristics:

> We may discern here descriptive poems, in which the Sufis tried to tell of their experiences in the mystical "states" (*aḥwāl*); technical poems with often complicated word plays, poems, and allusions; and popular poems which, as will become clear, often prefigure the mystical poetry in the non-Arabic areas.[45]

The range of styles employed in these poems attests to the heterogeneous character of Arabic Sufi poetry, which tentatively opened up a range of possibilities for poetic discourse, including the description of inner psychological states, the opaque exploration of coded terminology and wordplay, and bold emotional declarations that could be appreciated by a wider public. All of these characteristics are found in the poems attributed to Hallaj.

The literary forms of poetry that circulated in Sufi groups are indistinguishable from the standard forms of Arabic poetry in terms of rhyme, meter, and even subject matter. Much of this poetry is very brief, consisting of a few lines at most. Early Sufi poetry has at times been described as "little concerned with literary conventions,"[46] although in fact one can find plenty of examples of rhetorical flourishes typical of the 'Abbasid "new style" (*badi'*). The long and intricate odes (*qasidas*) that developed in pre-Islamic Arabia and were perfected by the poets of the early caliphate are not commonly found in early Sufi works; as Schimmel comments, "the classical form of the *qasida* with its traditional framework was used by them only much later."[47] It is possible that the classical odes were initially seen as too worldly, due to their courtly associations. Th. Emil Homerin has suggested that the first major step in this direction was taken by Ibn al-Shahrazuri (d. 1117), a Sufi who authored what may be the first major Arabic mystical poem written in the style of the *qasida*.[48]

The flowering of that complex literary form as a mystical genre would take place in the thirteenth century, in the prodigious *qasida* compositions of Ibn al-Farid (d. 1235) and Ibn `Arabi (d. 1240). As Denis McCauley points out, the early Arabic poetry found among Sufis generally lacks such refined and lengthy creations.[49] Sufis often recited poetry at communal gatherings featuring the ritual recitation of divine names (*dhikr*), where Sufi adepts engaged in the discipline of listening (*sama`*), often to musical accompaniment. For the most part, those poems were relatively straightforward, without complicated metaphysical references, and their impact was often manifest in the state of ecstasy attained by listeners. In contrast, Ibn `Arabi and Ibn al-Farid composed their long, intricate odes with the dense allusions typical of court poetry, often recalling the classical pre-Islamic ode, and generally aimed at (in the case of Ibn `Arabi at least) an audience of a restricted circle of intimate disciples rather than a wider public.[50] As for Ibn al-Farid, his poetry has taken on a liturgical popularity despite its difficulty.[51] In these respects, both Ibn `Arabi and Ibn al-Farid differ from the Andalusian Sufi al-Shushtari (d. 1269), whose verses drew on popular demotic Arabic rather than the conventions of the formal ode.[52]

In contrast with those later productions, most of the Hallajian corpus consists of the shorter occasional piece (*muqatta`a* or *qit`a*), which is usually concerned with a single topic.[53] The shortest pieces are only one or two lines, the latter resembling the quatrain (*ruba`i*) that would become standard in Persian literature. These stipulations underline the exceptional character of a dozen Hallajian poems identified by Massignon as full-fledged odes (*qasida*s), since they amount to ten lines or more on average (nos. 34, 44, 57, 70, 75, 78, 85, 86, 88, 89, 90, 114). These poems in fact demonstrate complex symmetrical structure and generally illustrate a process of transformation of the self, features that are typical of the category of the *qasida*.[54] Yet it is something of a stretch to confer the status of full-blown ode on these poems, most of which are relatively compact. It may have been the attraction of literary prestige that led Massignon to identify these poems as examples of the *qasida*.

While classical Arab literary critics did not recognize Sufi poetry as a separate genre, there are examples that indicate the perception that a particular style was characteristic of Sufis. As Homerin points out, the classical Arab poet al-Mutanabbi (d. 965) was criticized by the commentator al-Tha`alibi (d. 1038) for "imitating the expressions of the Sufis and using their tangled words of abstruse meanings." Another commentator remarks that al-Mutanabbi seemed to have taken a particular expression "from the style (*tarz*) of Sufi speech," specifically quoting a verse by Hallaj as an example.[55] What these critics seem to have had in mind was the "intricate and sophisticated style . . . characterized by antithesis (*tibaq*), paronomasia (*jinas*), and the repetition of verbs and an abundance of prepositions in contrast and opposition within a single verse."[56] While this account clearly recalls Hallaj's style, the poetry it describes is a logical development following the Sufis' formation of a technical language for mystical experience. Schimmel draws attention to how "the Sufis skillfully used their recently developed technical vocabulary and played on all the possible derivations of Arabic words, with their three radical consonants, to attain a highly complicated web of words which could be disentangled only by the initiate."[57] As an example, there are several places in Hallaj's poetry where prepositions pile up disconcertingly to obliquely indicate that all things must be simultaneously connected to God. In poem 114, Hallaj is arguing against the philosophers who believe that God is the first cause that is known by reason from his effects; Hallaj insists that, to the contrary, God is only known through himself: "One doesn't prove the Creator by his work; / have you seen a creature reveal the times? // The proof was for him, from him, to him, by him, / from Truth's witness in a scripture's descent." Occurring in the midst of a poem, his clustered prepositions effectively summarize a much more complex argument (similar expressions are found in poems 70 and 84).

While the point of these verses may appear intuitively clear through the use of simple language, they actually demonstrate Hallaj's mastery over the emerging technical vocabulary of Sufism. This mystical jargon was not always admired, as one can see in this anecdote about the Baghdadian Sufi Abu al-`Abbas Ibn `Ata', who ended up being killed by the caliph's police for his support of Hallaj:

> Some of the theologians said to Ibn `Ata, "What is it with you Sufis, that you deconstruct words so that they are strange to the ear of listeners, and you abandon customary language? This only has two outcomes: either you're distorting things, or in God most high no distortion takes place. So it must be the case that in your teaching there is an external flaw that you conceal from people with [these] words." Ibn `Ata said, "We do this because it empowers us, because this activity is dear to us; we didn't want anyone else besides this group to know it, and we didn't want to employ ordinary, common words, so we invented special words."[58]

The technical vocabulary of Sufism was in fact collected in the form of dictionaries of mystical terms, which were distributed in Sufi circles.[59] It is striking that the very first definition in the Sufi lexicon of Sarraj is identical in form with the piled-up prepositions in Hallaj's poem:

> And the meaning of their saying, "the Truth, by the Truth, for the Truth": Now "the Truth" is God, for in the Qur'an commentary of Abu Salih on the verse "and if the Truth had followed their desires" [Qur'an 23:71], he said "the truth is God most high." Abu Sa`id al-Kharraz said in some of his sayings, "the devotee is dependent with the Truth, by the Truth, for the Truth"; that is, with God, by God, for God. There-fore, "from him, by him, for him" means from God, by God, for God.[60]

This is precisely the language employed by Hallaj and other Sufis in their poetry, as well as in their prose writings. In poem 85, in which the first five verses are essentially a list of Sufi technical terms, Hallaj remarks that "These are expressions for the people to whom / the world is equivalent to a penny." Louis Massignon rightly drew attention to the decisive role that Hallaj played in the elaboration of Sufi terminology, and it is not accidental that Hallaj's vocabulary forms the core of Massignon's *Essay on the Origins of the Technical Language of Islamic Mysticism*.

Beyond these formal characteristics, it is important to locate Sufi poetry in the social context of where it was performed and of the audience that listened to it. In modern scholarship, the mystic is often seen in a timeless fashion, as by definition this figure is centered on the eternal and infinite source: the mystical poem expresses a state of spiritual absences or separations on the one hand or realization of essential unity with God on the other.[61] As Th. Emil Homerin points out, however, it is important to step back from modern romantic concepts of the poet as an isolated figure expressing private senti-ments through a direct transcription of personal experience:

> Many medieval and modern readers have viewed this poetry as verse accounts of Sufi doctrine reflecting a mystic's endeavors to describe an experience of great profundity and overwhelming emotion. Yet, too of-ten, such explanations are based on romantic notions of poetry that focus on an individual's lonely self-struggle, and they isolate this poetry from its larger social, religious, and literary context. . . . Mystical verse, then, is as much a collective as an individual vision of reality that interprets human existence in order to imbue life with sense and significance.[62]

Although the extent of early Arabic Sufi poetry is not large, it is evident that, particularly in the eastern lands, it was commonly recited in community: in sessions where music was performed and ecstasy was a common phenomenon.

On a more profound level, the individualistic perception of mysticism fails to do justice to the deeply felt sense of community that plays a strong role in Hallaj's poetry. Despite the ambivalence with which Sufis viewed him, Hallaj clearly saw his own path as inseparable from the vision articulated within the Sufi community. In poem 114, "Theory of Existence," he calls proof of God a "truth that we discovered. . . . This is the true finding of his ecstatic seekers, / the like-minded—my friends and companions." In the lengthy "Letter from the Depth of Spirit" (no. 13), Hallaj swears "by the truth's truth of the faithful," proclaiming that "you all became my homeland." Elsewhere (no. 70) he describes God as "the One whose martyrs are alive," though they "become humbled in their longing." From their esoteric standpoint, these Sufis can see the world as worthless (no. 85), yet they "stray and wander" even after God shows himself to them (no. 109). In the end, "He settles his friends in his vicinity, / with wonderful grace and beautiful freshness" (no. 84). Elsewhere (in no. 109), Hallaj calls the community of Sufis "people of a secret, created for secrets," in a very frank expression of the conflict that Hallaj created; as the Persian poet Hafiz later wrote, "That friend by whom the gallows were ennobled—his crime was this: he made the secrets public."[63] Yet, after he reveals his paradoxical experiences, Hallaj can rejoice in his reception: "Certain youths know now what I have learned, for they / are my friends, since the good have friendship" (no. 88).

More generally, many examples could be cited to demonstrate the significance of poetry in the early Sufi community, but the following instance provides an admirable illustration:

> It is related of Abu al-Husayn al-Nuri (may God have mercy on him) that he gathered with a group of shaykhs by invitation, and a discussion took place among them regarding religious knowledge. Abu al-Husayn al-Nuri fell silent, then he raised his head and recited these verses:

> > Many a cooing dove at dawn
> > > chanted a lament in the thicket
> > And my weeping may have affected her
> > > and her weeping may have affected me
> > But if she complains, I don't understand
> > > and if I complain, she doesn't understand—
> > Unless I know her by passion,
> > > and she, too, knows me by passion.

> There was not a single person in the group who did not rise and go into ecstasy when al-Nuri recited these verses.[64]

There are several points about the story that claim our attention. First of all there is the remarkable depiction of Nuri either recalling or, more probably, extemporaneously composing verses to respond to a scholarly dilemma. Then there is the fact that the imagery of the poem is exceedingly conventional in terms of early Arabic poetry. The invocation of the dove as the model of a complaining lover is typical, and it is enhanced here by the claim of an empathetic relationship between the poet and the dove, which at first is unfortunately limited by their mutual incomprehension. But then all limitations are exploded by an immersion in passion, which creates an instant understanding between the complaining dove and the lover. While there is no overt reference to any mystical topic in this poem, the effect is unmistakable: all those present stood and entered into empathetic ecstasy (*tawajud*) simply upon hearing about the dramatic empathy described in the poem. Such mystical emotion is crucial to the Sufi practice of listening to poetry and music. This is far from an isolated example of the deep resonance of conventional Arabic poetry in Sufi circles. The great Persian poet Rumi, who himself was steeped in the Arabic poetic tradition, quoted similar verses by an Umayyad poet, verses describing the emotional interaction between a poet and a dove, in the preface to book IV of his *Mathnawi*.[65]

So it is impossible to separate Sufi poetry from the other kinds of literary production that flourished in the early `Abbasid era. Several vignettes from Sarraj's account of Sufi writers illustrate the range of poetic registers that occur in Sufi literature. Sarraj comments at length on the practice of letter writing among Sufis, indicating the prominence of this activity as an intimate form of communication between like-minded spiritual aspirants: "Al-Junayd wrote a letter to Mumshad al-Dinawari, and when it reached him, he turned it over and wrote what he wrote on the back: 'Only a correct one to a correct one, and the two do not differ in reality.'"[66] Evidently poetry was frequently both a topic and a medium in such correspondence, as one can see in a letter from Khalid al-Suri, who said,

> I wrote a letter to Abu `Ali al-Rudhbari, in which were these lines:
>
> > My secrecy, Abu `Ali, is for my love
> >   of you, fleeing from sharing it.
> > How happy you are, town of Rudhbar! What right
> >   do you have over us? Without him, you are a desert.
>
> Then he received me for some days, and I had a piece of paper in my hands. He took it from my hands and wrote on the back:

> Love incited you to love; in its frustration
>> there is a heavenly grace, and in its blame is an attraction.
> Master of passions! From a well with no return
>> you've enjoyed pure desire, but not its goal.
> Stand beneath his bench with your affection for him,
>> infatuated in anxious sufferings for him![67]

What is striking in this exchange of verses, which receives no further comment from Sarraj, is the artful invocation of the complex conceits found in love poetry, combined with the very physical practice of writing as an intimate communication—what one Arab critic calls "the experience of writing, and the writing of experience."[68] Indeed, the very image of writing appears in highly conventional lyrics of Sufis like Abu ʿAli al-Rudhbari:

> I wrote to you with the tears of my eyes,
>> and my heart was drenched with the water of desire.
> My hand inscribes, and my heart is not fatigued,
>> but my eyes erase whatever those have written.[69]

This embodiment of love poetry in letters will find expression in the correspondence between Hallaj and his close friend and supporter Ibn ʿAta' (poems 29 and 101), who are both found in narratives that depict the intimate exchange of poetry in written letters (see appendix 3).

By its very nature, therefore, the poetry recited in Sufi circles cannot be separated from the verses recited in more worldly settings. Indeed, the texts can be the same in both cases. As Sarraj concedes, "One who undertakes to listen to these quatrains belongs to one of two perspectives: either distracted people among the frivolous and contentious, or the people who have attained noble states, embraced pleasing stations, mortified their souls with austerities and struggles, cast aside the world beyond their manifestation, and concentrated on almighty God in all their thoughts."[70] This is a striking acknowledgment that some poems circulating among the Sufis also appealed to very different audiences in slightly different forms. And this was not just a case of Sufis being fond of Abu Nuwas. A verse attributed to Hallaj turns out to be an adaptation of some lines by an early ʿAlid leader.[71] Even the famous poem on the "two loves," commonly viewed as written by Rabiʿa of Basra (d. 810), one of the earliest woman Sufis, has been shown to be based on lines by an early Umayyad poet.[72]

Immediately preceding the exchange between Rudhbari and Suri that was described above, Sarraj relates a story about the presence of worldly poetry in Sufi circles:

I was in Ramla, and a Hashemite man was there who owned a famous singing girl with a beautiful voice and elegant speech. So we asked Abu `Ali al-Rudhbari to write a message to him asking permission to visit her, so we could hear something from her. So in my presence he immediately wrote, "In the name of God the Merciful, the Compassionate! It has reached me—may God answer your request, and give you your hopes—that you have one of the resorts of refreshment, where the hearts of the people of ecstasy alight, so they can drink from it with the vessels of faithfulness, a wine bequeathed them by the realities of purity. And if we are permitted to enter it, then for us it is incumbent on the master of the resort that he should beautify the assembly by excluding others, and veil it from gazing eyes; our coming is dependent on your permission. Farewell."[73]

We are not told the outcome of this elliptical request, which is expressed in elegant and formal rhyming prose. Contrary to the strict gender seclusion typically enjoined by Sufi manuals for regulating the practice of listening to poetry and music, this anecdote indicates that Sufi adepts could find professional singing girls attractive for the performance of poems that invoke "the realities of purity"—although privacy might be necessary to avoid social complications! The use of key Sufi terminology for inner states of ecstasy is nevertheless linked in the letter with the wine imagery that was integral to secular court culture.

Another story related by Sarraj connects poetry to the deeper cosmic forces linking humanity and nature:

I heard al-Junayd (God's mercy upon him) say, Sari al-Saqati handed me a letter, saying, "This is the place for your fulfilling my wish." So I opened the letter and in it was written,

I heard the camel driver in the desert calling out and saying,
"I weep, but do you know what makes me weep?
I weep from worry that you will depart from me
and end my union and exile me."[74]

The verses contained in the letter obliquely request an intimate friend not to leave. The supposed context for this brief account is the figure of the camel driver, who by this time was legendary for reciting poetry to urge his steeds through the desert; these conventional love lyrics, when combined with the power of the melodious human voice, were understood to have such an effect that even animals respond eagerly to it. This became a familiar theme in Sufi literature, and Sarraj elsewhere relates in fuller detail the tragicomic story of the camel driver whose voice is so beautiful that he drives his master's camels to their deaths.[75] Nor is that the only case in Sufi literature where ecstatic death results from listening to recited poetry.[76]

So we return to the question of whether one can discern a Sufi aesthetic when it comes to poetry. The problem is that the poetry that circulated in Sufi circles in many ways cannot be distinguished, in textual or formal terms, from other forms of poetry found in early Arab culture. In other words, although Sufi poetry commonly contains certain formal characteristics, it cannot be necessarily defined as the composition of particular authors nor even as a definite style or literary genre. Instead, the reception and interpretation of this poetry are what connect it to Sufism. Sufi poetry might then be defined as poems that are listened to and understood through the hermeneutics of Sufism, regardless of their origins or authorships. Far from specifying a formal genre, then, we are recognizing a milieu in which certain literary practices are performed with a variety of styles of poetry.

It is important to emphasize this performative dimension and its psychological impact as defining features of early Sufi literature in its aesthetic dimension. One may in fact stipulate that poetry is more of an aural phenomenon, since in Sufi texts much of the discussion of poetry is linked to the experience of listening. (As in many cultures, reciting poetry aloud would have been the norm, rather than silent reading.) It is noteworthy that music or the production of sound itself does not feature as a topic in manuals of Sufi practice; it is listening (*sama'*) that forms the central concern of early Sufi literature, rather than the visual dimension that has been highlighted in the aesthetics of later Sufi poetry.[77] In the earliest specialized Arabic text devoted to this question of listening, Abu 'Abd al-Rahman al-Sulami (d. 1021) explains how the capacity of the listener determines the experience of the text that is heard, whether the text is the Qur'an or poetry:

> Junaid said, "Listening is from the perspective of the listener, and therefore the most lawful thing that the listener listens to is the Qur'an, because it is a remedy, a mercy, a guidance, and a clarification. And the lowliest thing he can listen to is poetry—but perhaps listening to the Qur'an may be obscure to its listener, even though it is a remedy and a mercy, and it may be that poetry is a wisdom in the heart of the listener, even if it is foolishness in itself." . . . So the one who realizes the truth in listening hears the false as true, and the one who does not realize the truth in it hears the truth as false.[78]

There is an obviously apologetic tone in Sulami's defense of poetry, as he brings in the unimpeachable Sufi master Junayd to bolster the case for listening to poetry. But in his next comment, Sulami introduces the classic example of Sufi hermeneutics, a story usually ascribed to Abu Hulman, who heard a Baghdad street vendor shouting out the name of the herbs he was selling: "O country thyme (*ya sa`tara al-barri*)!" Abu Hulman fell down in a faint, and when he was asked later for an explanation, he said that he had understood instead, "At the Hour [of Resurrection], you will see my piety (*al-sa`at tara birri*)!"[79] Regardless of what was actually said by the street vendor, the Sufi understood a message aimed directly at him, and he was overwhelmed by the thought of his inadequacy to face God directly. There are numerous examples in Sufi literature of an adventitious warning coming from seemingly random stimuli. For Sulami, this variable hermeneutic meant that listeners could be divided into separate categories. According to this division, the ordinary masses should be prohibited from listening to poetry, because they would understand it in inappropriate ways; in contrast, the same texts were permitted or recommended to Sufi disciples and adept mystics, who could interpret them in a spiritual fashion.

In a similar vein, Sarraj concludes his chapter on poetry with these reflections about poetry's interpretation:

> In these poems some things are difficult and some things are clear, and there are subtle allusions and delicate meanings. Whoever looks at them should contemplate them so that he comprehends their aims and their secrets, so that he does not associate their author with anything inappropriate to them. But if this is difficult for him and he does not understand, he should seek the explanation by questioning one who does understand, since there is a theory for every station and an expert for every science; but if we pursued this clarification, the book would be too long![80]

The implications are clear: Sufi poetry is definable only in the interpretive context where the Sufi mentality holds sway.

As for the poems attributed to Hallaj, there is much that is distinctive about them. Key terms in the vocabulary of Hallaj include, appropriately, "truth" (*haqq*), the divine attribute he is said to have identified with; it occurs over thirty times. Also frequent is reference to God as "all" (*kull*), reflecting a sense of cosmic immanence. There are religious formulas of blessing (nos. 10 and 14) as well as oaths (nos. 13, 74, and 78). Hallaj recurrently depicts the suffering of love as prison, disease, poison, emaciation, and death, images that are also common in court poetry. The critics who blame lovers are often refuted. Hallaj frequently refers to the ocean (nos. 13, 24, 39, 49, 76, 78, 88, and 89) and the experience of drowning to indicate annihilation of the self, although he also uses the image of the desert (nos. 86 and 89) for a similar purpose. He employs symbolism of ascension and flight (nos. 67, 86, and 89) to describe the human approach to the divine, as well as the mixing of substances as a metaphor for union (nos. 100, 104, and 105). The tone of the poems is intimate, as most of the poems are addressed to a singular "you," although frequently the author complains about God, or praises him, to the reader. Iblis, the Islamic equivalent of Satan, takes on a particular importance for Hallaj as the true monotheist and faithful lover of God (nos. 20, 21, 41, and 99). At times Hallaj describes himself with an arresting image, as the one whose heart is seized in the claws of a bird (no. 86) or as the drowning man whose fingertips are the only remaining visible sign of him (no. 75). As the Spanish translators Milagros Nuin and Clara Janés point out, this is "poetry of the absolute interior rather than of intro-spection," with a subtle and highly developed terminology for the multiple aspects of mind and heart, and numerous variations on the different phases of love.[81]

So to what extent does Hallaj's poetry fit the pattern of the early Sufi literary practice? His verses are indeed intensely cerebral, filled with par-adoxes and punning uses of multiple prepositions; they have also been described as "words of unforgettable beauty."[82] At the same time, these poems demonstrate a thorough mastery over the emerging theological vocabulary of Islamic thought, which drew heavily on the Greek philosoph-ical tradition. Sometimes condemned by Arab literary critics as "tangled words," his verses nonetheless provide powerful expressions of ineffable states of union and separation; his poetry overlaps with the forms of stan-dard erotic poetry even as it "ruptures the psychological barriers of space, time, and rationality."[83] Many of these verses are unforgettably embedded in narratives (Akhbar al-Hallaj) that either prophesy or recount Hallaj's mar-tyrdom, placed alongside his prayer orations in rhyming prose. And these poems have only been preserved because they resonated with Sufi ideals and practice. So in terms of their style, vocabulary, and subject matter, the poems attributed to Hallaj are indeed characteristic of "poetry according to the path of Sufism."

The Question of Authorship

To what extent can we be confident about the authorship of poems atttributed to Hallaj? Frequently, early Sufi writers quote poetry with no concern for who the author may have been as long as the sentiment and the insight are appropriate to the subject at hand.[84] But when poetry itself becomes the subject, authorship comes to the fore. As an example, Abu Nasr al-Sarraj in his *Book of Glimmerings on Sufism* has a dense little chapter entitled "On Their Poetry and the Meanings of Their States and Hints."[85] This chapter contains scores of lines of poetry, usually in no more than four to six verses at a time, in the familiar Arabic form of the occasional verse (known as *muqqata`a* or *qit`a*) consisting of two-part lines (*bayt*s) with end rhyme. But in most cases Sarraj is able to quote the author or even the circumstances in which the author recited the verses to another notable Sufi. The case is similar with Abu Sa`d al-Khargushi of Nishapur (d. 1016) in his compendium *The Purification of Consciences in the Principles of Sufism*, where he also provides a handy chapter entitled "On the Recollection of Certain Types of Their Poems That They Recite."[86] Here the samples are evenly spread between anonymous poems and those attributed to particular authors. Sirjani (d. 1077), in his book *The White and the Black of the Particular Wisdom of God's Servants, Concerning the Attributes of the Disciple and the Master*, likewise has a chapter entitled "Recollection of the Poems by Which the Sufis Have Indicated the Manifestation of a State or the Answer to a Question."[87] Again, in most cases Sirjani provides not only the names of the authors of these poems but also the context of a conversation, or a question, to which each poem provides a conclusion. So it seems that, at least in certain contexts, Sufis could be quite clear about the authorship of particular poems.

From a contrary perspective, it might be assumed that the question of authorship would not be central in a tradition such as Sufism, which at least in theory is dedicated to the elimination of the ego. In this respect, it would be similar to the question of sainthood: in early Sufi writings the question arose whether the saint (whose ego was annihilated) would even be aware of being a saint. Paradoxically, this theoretical problem did not seem to bother some Sufis at all in practice. One of the great interpreters of Hallaj, the Persian poet `Attar, went to the extent of announcing, "Till the resurrection, no one as selfless as I will ever write verse with pen on paper!"[88] Perhaps because of the boldness of his claim to selflessness, the authorship of works attributed to `Attar has become a thorny question, and it has been suggested that a second or even a third person of the same name may have authored some of the writings attributed to him.[89] From a postmodern perspective, based on readings of Roland Barthes and Michel Foucault, Sufi poetry may be seen as an interauthorial and intertextual process that does not easily fit into the concept of individual authorship that has been so cherished in traditional literary criticism.[90]

Nevertheless, it is noteworthy that the early Sufi writer Hujwiri complained at length about the problem of plagiarism in the opening pages of his classic Sufi treatise *Revelation of the Mystery*:

> Two considerations have impelled me to put my name at the beginning of the book: one particular, the other general. As regards the latter, when persons ignorant of this science see a new book, in which the author's name is not set down in several places, they attribute his work to themselves, and thus the author's aim is defeated, since books are compiled, composed, and written only to the end that the author's name may be kept alive and that readers and students may pronounce a blessing on him. This misfortune has already befallen me twice. A certain individual borrowed my poetical works, of which there was no other copy, and retained the manuscript in his possession, and circulated it, and struck out my name which stood at its head, and caused all my labor to be lost. May God forgive him! I also composed another book, entitled "The Highway of Religion" (*Minhaj al-Din*), on the method of Sufiism—may God make it flourish! A shallow pretender, whose words carry no weight, erased my name from the title page and gave out to the public that he was the author, notwithstanding that connoisseurs laughed at his assertion. God, however, brought home to him the unblessedness of this act and erased his name from the register of those who seek to enter the divine portal.
>
> As regards the particular consideration, when people see a book, and know that its author is skilled in the branch of science which it treats, and is thoroughly versed therein, they judge its merits more fairly and apply themselves more seriously to read and remember it, so that both author and reader are better satisfied.[91]

Thus for Hujwiri, establishing true authorship was critically important, whether it concerned poetry or prose. In this respect, he shared the general attitude found in early Arabic poetry, where plagiarism (known in Arabic as *sariqa*, or theft) was both well-known and widely denounced; major anthologists of poetry, such as Abu al-Faraj al-Isbahani (author of the massive *Book of Songs*), were scrupulous and systematic in determining who was the correct author of any given piece of poetry.[92]

With Hallaj the situation seems a bit different, since people were not always eager to quote him by name, due to his notoriety. The tenth-century Sufi author Abu Bakr Kalabadhi referred obliquely to Hallaj as "one of the great ones" (*ba`d al-kibar*), cautiously citing him this way over sixty times (sometimes at considerable length) in the *Book of Recognition*, his famous treatise on Sufi teaching; there, only twice did Kalabadhi refer to Hallaj by one of his nicknames, Abu al-Mughith.[93] Comparison with other sources confirms that many of these quoted passages are otherwise known to be by Hallaj. Eight of Kalabadhi's citations are poems, and Massignon included three of these in his edition of the *Diwan*.[94] If Kalabadhi felt the need to be circumspect while writing in Bukhara only a few decades after Hallaj's death, later Sufi writers were not so cautious. Isma`il Mustamli Bukhari (d. 1043), Kalabadhi's successor in Bukhara a half century later, sprinkled a number of overt references to Hallaj in his Persian commentary on Kalabadhi's work.[95]

But controversy is not the only reason for questionable attribution of Sufi poetry; throughout early Arabic literature, it is fairly common for any single poem to be credited to several different authors. In the case of Hallaj, Massignon identified eighteen poems attributed to Hallaj that he judged to be by earlier authors, another five he judged to be by later authors, and twenty-one he believed were by anonymous authors imitating the style of Hallaj, in addition to the poems he deemed to be authentic. While one might want to quibble with some of these judgments, Massignon's conclusion is not necessarily idiosyncratic. The early Sufi author Sirjani, in his extensive manual of Sufism, quotes eleven poems found in Massignon's *Diwan* but attributes three of them to other Sufis.[96] Such authorial instability is hardly unusual in the history of Arabic literature, despite the desire for certainty. As one scholar observes,

> Paradoxically, the situation in regard to the texts of the early 'Abbāsid poets is often much worse than those of the Umayyad poets, since the philologists (who did not regard them as reliable authorities for linguistic usage) made no efforts to collect their *dīwāns*. Some have never been collected, and such *dīwāns* as survive in later manuscripts (including that of Abū Nuwās) are far from reliable. The authorship of single verses and even of whole poems is sometimes in question, and later collectors of *badī*ʿ [rhetorical] figures have caused much confusion by lack of care in citation and attribution.[97]

Despite the general interest in establishing legitimate claims to authorship, there were plenty of cases where such claims were disputed or unclear.

To this complicated issue of authorship one should add the attribution to Hallaj of a substantial volume of Persian poems that is still in circulation.[98] His supposed relationship to this volume appears to be impossible, however; reports in Sufi writings indicate that Hallaj (despite his Iranian ancestry) did not know Persian, since he was unable to understand the Persian conversation of `Ali ibn Sahl al-Isfahani.[99] In addition, Persian poetry had barely begun to be written down in Arabic script during Hallaj's lifetime, and there are no significant Sufi-oriented Persian poetic collections from that time. This pseudonymous Persian *Divan-i Mansur Hallaj* has been persuasively attributed to the authorship of a much later figure, Husayn Khwarizmi (d. 1435), whose pen name "Husayn" was also by coincidence the given name of Hallaj, in this way encouraging the confusion.[100]

All this goes to show that when it comes to establishing the "authentic" poems of Hallaj and distinguishing them from the merely "attributed" verses, there is plenty of room for debate. While some editors may confidently brandish the asterisk to label certain poems inauthentic, there is no manuscript evidence that can furnish undoubted proof about the authorship of Arabic verses written over a thousand years ago. Ultimately the matter evidently comes down to a question of judgment, depending on the way in which a particular editor or translator understands the authorial persona of Hallaj. A good example of this is poem 8, "Religion of Lovers, and Religion of the People," which is almost certainly not by Hallaj; it is a sentimental and highly conventional love poem with none of the mystical insights one would expect from Hallaj. This same poem was quoted by Hujwiri as an anonymous piece that he had heard from a passing dervish, who expired on the spot after reciting it; then a late Persian author claimed (contrary to all other evidence) not only that these were verses by Hallaj but also that they were his last words as he walked to the gallows. Whether because of this dramatic embellishment or just because he liked the poem, Louis Massignon insisted on identifying it as an "authentic" poem by Hallaj, a decision that has been cautiously followed by later editors. Remarkably, the same poem has circulated on YouTube as an anonymous devotional song addressed to the Prophet Muhammad, even becoming a popular hit in a widely viewed Ramadan television serial drama. I include it in this collection not because it has a convincing claim to be one of Hallaj's compositions but because it is part of the reception history associated with his writings, thus illustrating the difficulty of assigning authorship for his works with any certainty.

Hallaj and Massignon

The Iraqi scholar Kamil Mustafa al-Shaybi began his commentary on the poems of Hallaj with the following remarks:

> I was told by the Iraqi priest Father Dahan al-Mawsili, a resident of Paris, that the late Professor Louis Massignon . . . told him in the spring of 1953 to perform a special mass to the spirit of al-Husayn ibn

Mansur al-Hallaj, in the church which he supervised in the French capital, on the day of the memorial of his death, on the twenty-fourth of Dhi al-Qiʿda 309 hijri (March 26, 922 CE). And the priest Dahan recalled that he had been astonished at the request, and he reminded Professor Massignon that Hallaj was a Muslim, and the church was the house of Christian worship, but he replied, "Hallaj was a spiritual man and a Sufi, and the divisions of religions do not count for anything in his state."[101]

Shaybi went on to relate several anecdotes about Massignon and his extraordinary devotion to Hallaj, told with some amazement by an Iraqi Christian monk. As a result, he observed, "it is not strange, but rather natural, that we dedicate our efforts in the editing of the poems of Hallaj, and its commentary, to the late great Orientalist Professor Louis Massignon, who passed away to the spiritual world and encountered the witness of eternity, al-Husayn ibn Mansur al-Hallaj."[102] Who was Louis Massignon, the subject of this remarkable encomium, and what was his connection to Hallaj?

It must be acknowledged that much of what is known about Hallaj is owed to Massignon.[103] A number of commentators have held forth on the significance of Massignon's discovery of Hallaj in 1908 in a spiritual crisis in Baghdad, and his subsequent lifelong obsession, which may be tracked through a series of publications over half a century. There are those who view Massignon primarily through the lens of Catholic spirituality, given the fact that he was a Franciscan tertiary with a special dispensation from the pope to perform his liturgy in Arabic.[104] Others have instead considered him in the context of his struggle with his acknowledged homosexuality.[105] Massignon has also been criticized as an Orientalist who read his own Christian identity crisis onto a forgotten, marginal figure from the distant past.[106]

Be that as it may, it is nonetheless difficult to dismiss the intensity of Massignon's encounter with Hallaj.[107] Briefly, it appears that Louis Massignon first heard the story of the Sufi martyr from a young Spaniard convert to Islam with whom he had become infatuated. Then, while serving with a French archaeological expedition in Iraq in 1908, Massignon got lost in the desert, and in his wandering he encountered a spiritual presence that he somehow identified with both Jesus Christ and Hallaj. Subsequently found and given hospitality by an Iraqi family with a tradition of devotion to Hallaj, Massignon recovered and found purpose in reconstructing Hallaj's life and teachings, remaining dedicated to this task until his death in 1962. The milestones of his accomplishments include a series of publications of Arabic texts by and about Hallaj, as well as an important study on the technical terminology of Islamic mysticism.[108] The major synthesis that Massignon offered as testimony was *La Passion de Hallaj* (henceforth referred to in this text as *The Passion of Hallaj*), technically a doctoral dissertation despite its length of nearly a thousand pages—and coincidentally published in 1922, the millennial anniversary of the execution of Hallaj in 922. This monumental study comprised a detailed biography of Hallaj, lengthy explorations of his influence on later Sufis in multiple cultural environments, and an analysis of Hallaj's theological and legal contributions to Islamic thought and practice. Massignon continued to work on this vast project for the rest of his life. His accumulated notes resulted in a second edition, produced under the supervision of academic colleagues and family members in 1975 and twice as long as the first edition (two thousand pages in four volumes). The entire work was translated into English by Massignon's associate Herbert Mason in 1981.[109]

Despite Massignon's extraordinary labors and accomplishments, his lifelong dedication to Hallaj remained an unfinished project. On a very practical level, *The Passion of Hallaj* is almost unreadable. Dense textual analyses trail off in footnotes that lead nowhere. Broad claims and intimations of Massignon's famous intuition often end up resembling unfinished "notes to self." The admission of Massignon's translator, Mason, is telling: "Often his very obsession with evidence, with truth itself, marred his performance as a biographer and historian, from a literary standpoint. *La Passion de Hallaj*, which he felt could not be translated in its first edition, since it was incomplete, has not improved as a readable literary work in its second edition."[110] As Massignon himself confessed, his approach to this subject was highly personal: "I annex even to historical facts the further meditations that they have suggested."[111] Indeed, it may be said that the core objective of Massignon's project was to establish a personal connection to Hallaj through the transmission of his words by trustworthy witnesses. He formulated this aim explicitly in (at the very least) four different sections of *Passion*.

The first of these is a lengthy opening historiographical sketch entitled "The Survival of Hallaj: A Chronological Tableau," which attempts to provide an exhaustive account of the impact of the teachings of Hallaj that have survived until today.[112] The second presentation of this oral transmission is a shorter summary entitled "Eight Testimonial Chains."[113] This detailed analysis mimics the structure of the oral transmission of the hadith sayings of the Prophet Muhammad, in this way taking on a canonical character; Massignon describes it as "the survival of this 'excommunicated saint' through thirty Muslim generations by means of 'chains of witnesses,' *asanid*, furthering his memory as a lifeline of hope, up to this very day."[114] Then Massignon becomes rhapsodic as he describes the charisma and dedication he saw in the transmission of Hallaj's teachings:

The slow growth, up to the full flowering, of this collective belief in the sanctity of Hallaj, in the efficacy of his intervention, *hic et nunc*, as a witness (*shahid*) close to God, on behalf of the Community for which he had died, and one of whose spiritual pillars (*abdal, budala'*) he had been, is conveyed, in the Sunnite milieu, by *isnad*s, or chains of transmission, giving the names of traditionists who were convinced enough to dare, at the risk of their liberty or their life, to transmit, from responsible *rawi*s, an account concerning Hallaj.[115]

While those stipulations concerned narrative or doctrinal accounts, Massignon devotes a third list to a "Genealogy of the Modern Hallajiya (to Sanusi, d. 1859)," focusing on the key ritual practice of Sufism, the pronunciation and recollection of the names of God (*dhikr*), thus establishing an ongoing link to Hallaj through spiritual lineages.[116]

Finally, Massignon provides a fourth summary by generations, called "Early Oral Transmission of Texts," recalling the classification of hadith transmitters along similar lines (i.e., Companions, Successors, Successors of the Successors, etc.).[117] Massignon begins this account by announcing the absolute necessity of ensuring this oral transmission's reliability:

> In accordance with the established practice in Islam regarding testimonial accounts—every conclusive authority for which [credit] is given to oral tradition (*riwaya*) and every credit denied the annotated text (*sahifa*)—a critique of Hallaj's texts requires, first of all, an examination of the list of authorized witnesses, arranged according to generation, who assumed personal responsibility for transmitting them to us or calling our attention to them.[118]

Massignon then arranges these transmitters into four classes, enumerating 125 who died within fifty lunar years after the death of Hallaj (by 970), 60 who died within one hundred lunar years (by 1019), 38 who died within two hundred years (by 1116), and 19 who died after 1116. After analyzing the various chains deriving from these early transmitters, Massignon concludes, "In my opinion, there exists a continuous Hallajian *isnad* in the oral testimonies of Hallaj that I received."[119] He then provides details of encounters with four individuals—in Baghdad in 1908, in Cairo in 1909, in Istanbul in 1911 and 1945, and in Ankara in 1928—in which he personally received oral testimonies of Hallaj. It is no exaggeration to say that the years of research that Massignon dedicated to this project were devoted to confirming the canonical authority of a sacred text—which is none other than the teachings of Hallaj as transmitted to him.

How did Massignon's lifelong obsession with Hallaj affect his edition of the poems of Hallaj? Massignon's portentous remarks in the 1931 first edition of the *Diwan al-Hallaj* indicate that he saw it as no ordinary book. He introduces the project innocently enough, with an academic definition of the Arabic word *diwan* as a literary term: "A diwan is a complete collection of the poetic works of an author, established by a literary critic, generally following the order of rhymes."[120] Notably, he describes his book as "an effort at reconstitution, edition, and translation," in effect recognizing the speculative nature of the publication.[121] Massignon was aware that a purely literary collection of Hallaj's poetry had never existed, and indeed one of Massignon's earliest publications had been the preliminary edition of *News of Hallaj* in 1914, in which many poems are found embedded in narratives.[122] He acknowledges this point grudgingly: "This was in an unexpected presentation, imposing on it the literary form of *maqamat* or 'seances,' which was born at that time. . . . But has it ever been completely disassociated, like a normal *diwan*, from the prose texts that comment on its verse?"[123] Nevertheless, the discovery of additional manuscripts containing the poems led Massignon to hypothesize a complicated process of literary formation (see appendix 4, "Editions and Translations of the *Diwan al-Hallaj*"), which he summarizes as follows:

> These manuscripts represent, we believe, successive refashionings for a very old opuscule, reedited a year or more after the execution of Hallaj, by his disciple Shakir b. Ahmad Baghdadi, before answering his call, and getting himself executed, for him, in his turn, in order to perpetuate the memorial of his master whose writings were condemned to be destroyed.[124]

The dramatic tone of these remarks leaves no doubt regarding Massignon's view of the *Diwan* as a sacred text, intimately involved with the martyrdom of Hallaj.

The impact of Massignon, a European Christian and Orientalist, on modern Arab thought has been considerable. Given that his writings on Hallaj were published during the high point of European colonialism, it is not surprising that Arab intellectuals have viewed him with ambivalence. After all, Muslim tradition was deeply divided over Hallaj, who still remains controversial. While Massignon was widely admired for his sympathetic engagement with Sufism and Islam, he was also viewed with suspicion as an Orientalist who appropriated Islamic culture for his own purposes.[125] One Arab scholar sums up the dilemma with this question: "Shall we leave Hallaj to the Orientalists and dispense with him, or shall we defend him because he is one of us?"[126] Massignon's contributions and his relationship with Hallaj's writings remain highly personal and complex.

Despite his controversial reputation, Hallaj unquestionably had considerable impact on later authors in Arabic, Persian, Turkish, and other languages, a point that is amply demonstrated by Massignon in the second volume of *The Passion of Hallaj*. In modern times (again, due in good part to the Arabic texts published by Massignon), Hallaj has taken on a new popularity. This is particularly relevant to his Arabic poetry, since the preservation of the classical literary heritage means that these poems can be understood by anyone educated in Arabic, despite the fact that they are over a thousand years old. In good part, contemporary engagement with Hallaj does not represent anything like a continuous transmission of historic tradition, such as the "continuous Hallajian *isnad*" sought by Massignon; ironically, it is primarily through Massignon's publications that modern intellectuals have rediscovered Hallaj. A number of Arab singers have incorporated the poems of Hallaj into their repertoires, and one may encounter many of these musical versions in recordings on YouTube.[127] The Palestinian oud player Issa Boulos has recorded an entire album of compositions featuring Hallaj's poems.[128] But it is noteworthy that these singers employ the text of Massignon's edition of the *Diwan al-Hallaj* by default.

Among Arab authors, Hallaj has reemerged as a symbol of freedom and revolt against unjust power, as for instance in the prizewinning Arabic drama of Egyptian playwright Salah ʿAbd al-Sabur, *Maʾsat al-Hallaj* (*The Tragedy of Hallaj*), first performed in 1965. The title of the English translation was *Murder in Baghdad*, a nod to T. S. Eliot's *Murder in the Cathedral*; that drama on the martyrdom of Thomas Becket had in fact been a model for ʿAbd al-Sabur as he wrote his own play.[129] Another drama about Hallaj with a clear revolutionary emphasis was produced by Tunisian playwright ʿIzz al-Din al-Madani in 1973 under the title *Rihlat al-Hallaj* (*The Journey of Hallaj*).[130] Outside of the Arab world, the Toronto-based Modern Times Stage Company premiered the play *Hallaj*, by Soheil Parsa and Peter Farbridge, in 2009, with a return performance in 2011.[131] A clear sign of the renewed interest in Hallaj is demonstrated by a spate of new editions of his writings, particularly the *Diwan*, in the 1990s (see appendix 4). Major contemporary Arab poets such as ʿAbd al-Wahhab al-Bayati and Adunis have composed poems devoted to the personality of Hallaj.[132] Hallaj has also played a role in the modern Arabic novel.[133]

It is worth noting as well that a number of modern visual artists have been inspired by Hallaj in their work. The Iraqi artist Dia al-ʿAzzawi (b. 1939) composed pen-and-ink drawings inspired by the story of Hallaj.[134]

Shakir Hasan Al Sa'id (1926–2004), another Iraqi artist, contributed abstract compositions to accompany the poems in Kamil Mustafa al-Shaybi's editions of the *Diwan al-Hallaj*.[135] The Kurdish calligrapher Kakayi (b. 1959), who resides in Belgium, has created numerous graphic compositions based on the poetry of Hallaj, some of which he has gathered together in a short video called "Tribute to Al-Hallaj."[136] The prominent Turkish artist Erol Akyavaş (1932–1999), who was featured in a major retrospective exhibition at Istanbul Modern in 2013, had a strong engagement with the Sufi tradition, and several of his works explicitly invoke Hallaj (known in Turkish as Hallaci Mansur).[137] Akyavaş's calligraphic painting *Ene'l Hak* (the Turkish spelling of Hallaj's Arabic utterance *ana al-haqq*, "I am the Truth") set a new record for Turkish art when it sold at auction for 2.78 million lira in 2012.[138] Sweden-based Iraqi artist Amar Dawod held an exhibit of sketches and paintings inspired by the *Kitab al-Tawasin* of Hallaj at the Meem Gallery in Dubai from 2013 to 2014.[139] William Hart McNichols, a Jesuit priest and painter of Christian religious icons, has created an icon entitled *Islamic Mystic and Martyr al Hallaj*.[140] All these recent reconnections with the legacy of Hallaj arguably depend on the work of Louis Massignon as their mediating factor.

The Present Translation: Selection and Method

The present translation aims, as far as possible, for a clear and lucid expression in contemporary idiomatic English, with close attention to semantic integrity and attested reader receptions. I have also consulted, for comparison, translations of the poems into French (Massignon, Sami Ali, Stéphane Ruspoli), German (Schimmel), Persian (four translations), Spanish (Janés/ Nuin), and Urdu (Muzaffar Iqbal); details of those translations are provided in appendix 4. The aim of this book is to balance sound scholarship with an aesthetic presentation that works in the target language of English. Stylistically, the translation preserves elements of the original poem, using a page layout that maintains the verse structure of the original. A single verse represents the Arabic *bayt*, which is divided into two half verses or half lines (*misra'*). While in Arabic text editions these two-part verses are typically printed on a single typographic line if space permits, poems with longer verses are displayed on two lines. In this book, for consistency and symmetry, each verse is shown on two lines, the second of which is indented. To give an example, the following is a single verse:

> It's sad enough that I call to you persistently
> > as though I were distant, or you were hidden.

Although each verse occupies two physical lines, following common academic usage, the terms "verse" and "line" are used here interchangeably to denote the basic unit of Arabic poetry.[141] I have not attempted to imitate the original rhyme—that would be a daunting task in English due to its relative poverty in rhyme in comparison with Arabic, not to mention the fatigue induced by repeated rhyming verse. Nevertheless, the present translations offer an echo of the rhythms that animate the Arabic originals. The most important principle of translation, in my experience, is to clarify the logic of each poem's central metaphors, which are always accompanied and enhanced by parallelism and antithesis.

The arrangement of the traditional Arabic *diwan* or collected poems is alphabetical by end rhyme, which makes no sense for an English version. Instead, these translations are clustered in eight thematic groups: (I) Conventional Love Lyrics, (II) Mystical Love Poems, (III) Martyrdom, (IV) Metaphysics, (V) Prayers and Sermons, (VI) Riddles, (VII) The Spiritual Path, and (VIII) Union. Not every poem fits neatly into one category, but this organization of the poems aims to illustrate the range of composition in Hallaj's poetry.

While it would be tempting to present the poems in unadorned translations, that might not be a service to readers new to this material. Also, it is important to recall that the core manuscripts of the "poems and prayers" of Hallaj (which Qushayri and Hujwiri sought) placed them into a narrative context. With that in mind, I offer three levels of access to the poems. First is the full collection of 117 poems in translation, each of which is provided with a title and prefaced by a short introduction pointing out the main themes and structure. Second is a section of notes to all the poems, including first lines, source references, notes on transmitters of the poem, comments on textual problems, and significant variant readings; these notes to the translations include references to sources mentioned in the introductions to the poems, but full bibliographical details are best consulted in Shaybi's commentary on the poems. Third, appendix 3, "Staging the Poetry," presents twenty-two dramatic narratives from *News of Hallaj*, in each of which is embedded one of the poems, to provide an alternative reading experience based on each poem's most common traditional setting.

In terms of stylistic conventions for this book, diacritical marks for transliteration of Arabic terms are provided only in the notes, using the system of the *International Journal of Middle East Studies*. In referring to Arab names and book titles, diacritical marks are not used, and for convenience the definite article "al-" is usually dropped, so al-Hallaj is cited as Hallaj. Bibliographic references to Arabic or Persian publications may provide the date according to the Islamic lunar calendar (or, in the case of Iran, the solar hijri calendar), followed by a slash and then the equivalent date in the Gregorian calendar (for example, 1363/1984). In translating mystical poetry from a language that has no capital letters, it is impossible to be consistent with English rules for capitalizing pronouns referring to God; the use of "he" or "He" is therefore provisional and inherently ambiguous. The aim throughout is to provide a user-friendly and accessible text for the general reader as well as full details for the scholar.

The reception history of these poems has determined their meaning. For that reason, I have focused on the function of the poems in the ongoing Arabic literary tradition rather than on engaging in another archaeological expedition into the manuscripts. In this process, the very act of assigning authorship has hermeneutical consequences. To ascribe one of these poems (like no. 43, "My Drinking Buddy") to the ʿAbbasid court poet Abu Nuwas results in a very different interpretation than if one assumes it is by the Sufi martyr Hallaj. The notes to the poems indicate who have been the principal transmitters of the poetry of Hallaj. Fittingly, the Sufi masters Sulami and Qushayri found reason to quote a number of these poems in their commentaries on the Qur'an; that is an indication of the status of these verses in the formative period of Sufism.

The aim of these translations has not been to restore the authentic poems of Hallaj, which remain disputed. The controversy that inevitably is attached to his name and the normal uncertainties of authorship of short Arabic poems make that project impossible. For that reason, this collection makes no claim to be the "complete poems" of Hallaj. This selection is a relatively expansive modern canon, consisting of the eighty-nine poems included by Massignon in his second edition (ninety poems are listed in index 4, but M28 and M29 are treated as a single poem), plus twelve additional poems from the "registry" manuscripts and four quoted by Kalabadhi, initially rejected by Massignon but accepted by Shaybi. To these are added three (nos. 3, 92, and 116) listed as doubtful by most editors but included nonetheless, along with the nine poems discovered in a Shiraz manuscript by Fritz Meier (for details see appendix 4). It is this collection of 117 poems (a total of 512 lines) that I propose as a modern equivalent of the little red square booklet that Qushayri failed to steal over a thousand years ago.

Not all of the poems I have selected can be considered as undoubtedly the products of Hallaj's pen; in fact, some are certainly not. The judgment I have used, admittedly personal, rests on the recognition of an extraordinary voice that pervades the best of these Hallajian verses. If some of these poems turn out to have been written by others who have successfully expressed that voice, they deserve to be included. I have abstained, however, from adding another section of poems labeled as inauthentic; the point of this collection is to provide a satisfactory illustration of Hallaj's poetry rather than an exhaustive treatment.

On another level, while I acknowledge the fascination surrounding the poetry of Hallaj, I part ways from Massignon insofar as his project was a personal way to connect with a charismatic spiritual figure of the past. This translation is presented not as hagiography but as literature, and the poems are read as poems, not as theology, sacred text, or direct transcriptions of personal experience. While it is impossible to entirely separate the poems of Hallaj from the story of his martyrdom, one can temporarily bracket out those narratives and focus instead on the poems themselves as powerfully crafted literary productions.

This project is also intended as a contribution to deepening Americans' understanding of Islamic culture and the Middle East through literature. The tens of thousands of American soldiers who in recent years have been sent to Iraq evidently have had little acquaintance with the traditions of this ancient home of civilization. That is not surprising, but it does not have to stay that way. Ironically, it was just over a century ago (in 1908) that Louis Massignon, while serving in a French archaeological expedition outside Baghdad, was apprehended as a spy and had the experiences that led him to devote his academic career to the study of Hallaj, bringing him to the attention of European and American scholars. But the personal obsession of Massignon need not define Hallaj for others. If there is a voice that we can identify in these poems as Hallaj—and I believe I recognize such a voice—then it is worth making these poems from a thousand years ago available to new audiences.

Notes

1. Abu al-Qasim `Abd al-Karim al-Qushayri, *al-Risala al-Qushayriyya*, ed. `Abd al-Halim Mahmud and Mahmud ibn al-Sharif (Cairo: Dar al-Kutub al-Haditha, 1966), 486–87. Unless otherwise noted, all translations are mine.

2. The text entitled *The Cabinet on the Destruction of Eras* (*Kitab al-sayhur fi naqd al-duhur*), which Sulami offered as a substitute for Hallaj's poems and prayers, does not survive. It is presumably identical with the *Kitab al-sayhur*, of which a brief excerpt is preserved in Hebrew script, cited in Louis Massignon's *Essai sur les origines du lexique technique de la mystique musulmane*, nouvelle édition revue et considérablement augmentée (Paris: J. Vrin, 1968), 447. While Massignon translates *sayhur* as "umbra" (shadow), Arabic dictionaries (such as *Taj al-`arus*) only record it as meaning a cabinet of clay or wood for storing household implements. Al-Nadim refers to this title as *al-Sahyun* (see al-Husayn ibn Mansur Hallaj, *Diwan al-Hallaj: wa-yalihi akhbaruhu wa-tawasinuh*, 2nd ed., ed. Sa`di Dannawi [Beirut: Dar Sadir, 2003], 19) or *al-Sihun* (see *The Fihrist of Al-Nadim: A Tenth-Century Survey of Muslim Culture*, trans. Bayard Dodge [New York: Columbia University Press, 1970], 1:478, note 121). Qushayri's reference to the longer title, *Kitab al-sayhur fi naqd al-duhur*, suggests by its rhyme that al-Nadim's version is to be corrected accordingly (see appendix 2, no. 5).

3. Kalabadhi quotes Hallaj frequently in this anonymous fashion; see Abu Bakr al-Kalābādhī, *The Doctrine of the Ṣūfis. Kitāb al-taʿarruf li-madhhab ahl al-taṣawwuf*, trans. Arthur John Arberry (Lahore: Sh. Muhammad Ashraf, 1966), 16, 52, 53, 54, 76, 101, 105, 111, 117, 122, 126, 127, 131, 132, 146, 147, 148, 153, 157, 164, 173, 181.

4. ʿAli al-Hujwiri, *Revealing the Mystery (Kashf al-mahjub)*, trans. R. A. Nicholson (London: E. J. W. Gibb Memorial, 1911; repr., New York: Pir Press, 1999), 343–44. Page references are to the Pir Press reprint.

5. Ibid., 149–53.

6. Ibid., 260–61.

7. A collection of texts on Hallaj, ranging in tone from hostility to veneration, is found in Eric Schroeder, *Muhammad's People; a Tale by Anthology—The Religion and Politics, Poetry and Violence, Science, Ribaldry, and Finance of the Muslims, from the Age of Ignorance before Islam and the Mission of God's Prophet to Sophistication in the Eleventh Century; a Mosaic Translation* (Portland, Maine: Bond Wheelwright, 1955; repr., Mineola, N.Y.: Dover Publications, 2002), 521–54. Page references are to the Bond Wheelwright edition.

8. Louis Massignon, *The Passion of al-Hallaj, Mystic and Martyr of Islam*, trans. Herbert Mason, 4 vols. (Princeton: Princeton University Press, 1982), 1:4–18.

9. Massignon, *Passion*, 1:18–36.

10. Carl W. Ernst, *Words of Ecstasy in Sufism*, SUNY Series in Islam (Albany: State University of New York Press, 1985), 102–10.

11. Ibid., 14.

12. *Farid Ad-Din ʿAttār's Memorial of God's Friends: Lives and Sayings of Sufis*, trans. Paul Losensky (Mahwah, N.J.: Paulist Press, 2009), 394–408.

13. Ahmet T. Karamustafa, *Sufism, the Formative Period* (Edinburgh: Edinburgh University Press, 2007).

14. Abu Bakr Ahmad ibn ʿAli ibn Thabit al-Khatib al-Baghdadi, *Tarikh madinat al-salam*, ed. Bashar ʿAwwad Maʿruf, vol. 8 (1422; repr., Beirut: Dar al-Gharb al-Islami, 2001), 688–89.

15. Ruzbihan Baqli, *Mantiq al-asrar*, manuscript cataloged anonymously as *Tafsir al-shathiyyat bi-lisan al-sufiyya*, Tashkent State Institute of Oriental Studies, no. 3198, 47–49. This important passage was not translated in the Persian version of this text, the *Sharh-i shathiyat*.

16. Ruzbihan Baqli, *Sharh-i shathiyat*, ed. Henry Corbin (Tehran: Anjuman-i Īrān-shināsī-i Farānsah dar Tihrān, 1981), 455.

17. *Passion*, 3:270–76.

18. Hujwiri, *Revealing the Mystery*, 151.

19. These Arabic texts are transcribed in Massignon, *Essai*, 336–449; see also al-Hallaj, *Haqa'iq al-tafsir, aw, Khalq khala'iq al-Qur'an wa-al-iʿtibar*, ed. Mahmud al-Hindi (Cairo: Maktabat Madbuli, 2006).

20. Translated in *Passion*, 3:327–34.

21. Translated in *Passion*, 3:279–327. The Arabic text is cited according to "*Kitab al-tawasin*," ed. Paul Nwyia, *Mélanges de l'Université Saint-Joseph* 47 (1972), 185–237.

22. See particularly Kamil Mustafa al-Shaybi, *Sharh diwan al-Hallaj* (2nd ed., Cologne: Manshurat al-Jamal, 2007; repr., 2012), cited here as Shaybi²; this text edition with commentary is the most important source for the present translation.

23. Hujwiri, *Revealing the Mystery*, 344.

24. Al-Khatib al-Baghdadi, *Ta'rikh Baghdad*, ed. Mustafa `Abd al-Qadir `Ata (Beirut: Dar al-Kutub al-`Ilmiyya, 1997), 8:112 (no. 4232).

25. Kalabadhi, *The Doctrine of the Sufis*, 16–17, with minor modifications (changing archaic "thou sayest" to "you say"); see also al-Qushayri, *Epistle on Sufism*, 6–7.

26. *Al-Daylami's Treatise on Mystical Love*, trans. Joseph Norment Bell and Hassan Mahmoud Abdul Latif Al Shafie (Edinburgh: Edinburgh University Press, 2005), lvi–lvii.

27. Hallaj's passage on love is translated in Daylami, *Treatise on Mystical Love*, 39–43, corresponding to pp. 51–55 of the Arabic text. The latter is available in Abu al-Hasan `Ali ibn Muhammad al-Daylami, *Kitab `atf al-alif al-ma'luf `ala al-lam al-ma`tuf*, ed. Hassan Mahmoud Abdul Latif Al Shafie and Joseph Norment Bell (Cairo: Dar al-Kitab al-Misri, 2007).

28. Abú Nasr `Abdallah B. `Alí al-Sarráj al-Túsí, *The Kitáb al-Luma` fi 'l-Tasawwuf*, ed. Reynold Alleyne Nicholson, "E. J. W. Gibb Memorial" Series, vol. 22 (London, 1914; repr., London: Luzac & Company, 1963), 288.

29. Sulami, *Tabaqat al-Sufiyya*, 434, quoted in Martin Lings, "Mystical Poetry," in `*Abbasid Belles Lettres*, ed. Julia Ashtiany et al., The Cambridge History of Arabic Literature (Cambridge, U.K.: Cambridge University Press, 1990), 239.

30. Sir William Jones, "On the Mystical Poetry of the Persians and Hindus," in *The Works of Sir William Jones* (London: G. G. and J. Robinson, 1799),1:445–62.

31. Michael Sells, "The Qasida and the West: Self-Reflective Stereotype and Critical Encounter," *Al-`Arabiyya* 20, (1987): 307–57.

32. Reynold Alleyne Nicholson, *Studies in Islamic Mysticism* (Cambridge, U.K.: Cambridge University Press, 1921), 162–63.

33. P. F. Kennedy, "Zuhdiyya," *Encyclopaedia of Islam*, 2nd ed., ed. P. Bearman, Th. Bianquis, C. E. Bosworth, E. van Donzel, and W. P. Heinrichs, Brill Online, 2013, , accessed July 27, 2013.

34. Andras Hamori, "Love Poetry (Ghazal)," in `*Abbasid Belles Lettres*, ed. Ashtiany et al., 205–6.

35. Jean Claude Vadet, *L'Esprit courtois en Orient dans les cinq premiers siècles de l'Hégire* (Paris: G.-P. Maisonneuve et Larose, 1968).

36. Ewald Wagner, "Abū Nuwās," *Encyclopaedia of Islam*, 3rd ed., ed. Kate Fleet, Gudrun Krämer, Denis Matringe, John Nawas, and Everett Rowson, Brill Online, 2013, accessed July 27, 2013.

37. Hujwiri, *Revealing the Mystery*, trans. Nicholson, 406.

38. Ruzbihan Baqli, *Mantiq al-asrar*, 32; *Sharh-i shathiyyat*, 177.

39. Th. Emil Homerin, "Tangled Words: Toward a Stylistics of Arabic Mystical Verse," in *Reorientations: Arabic and Persian Poetry*, ed. Suzanne Pinckney Stetkevych (Bloomington: Indiana University Press, 1994), 191.

40. *Kitáb al-Luma`*, 275.

41. Abu Sa`d `Abd al-Malik ibn Muhammad ibn Ibrahim ibn Ya`qub al-Nisaburi al-Kharkushi, *Tahdhib al-asrar fi usul al-tasawwuf*, ed. Imam Sayyid Muhammad `Ali (Beirut: Dar al-Kutub al-`Ilmiyya, 2006), 457, also cited by Sarraj, *Kitáb al-Luma`*, 110, 387. The Persian name *Khargushi* is Arabicized as *Kharkushi*.

42. Michael Sells, "Return to the Flash Rock Plain of Thahmad: Two Nasībs by Ibn al-'Arabī," *Journal of Arabic Literature* 39 (2008): 3–13.

43. *Passion*, 2:128.

44. Al-Qushayri, *Epistle on Sufism*, 85, 172.

45. Annemarie Schimmel, *As through a Veil: Mystical Poetry in Islam* (New York: Columbia University Press, 1982), chapter 1, "Flowers of the Desert: The Development of Arabic Mystical Poetry," 11–48, quoting 18.

46. Lings, "Mystical Poetry," 249.

47. Schimmel, *As through a Veil*, 19.

48. Th. Emil Homerin, "A Distant Fire: Ibn Al-Shahrazūrī's Mystical Ode and Arabic Sufi Verse," *Journal of Sufi Studies* 4, no. 1–2 (November 13, 2015): 27–58, doi:10.1163 /22105956-12341275.

49. Denis Enrico McAuley, *Ibn `Arabi's Mystical Poetics* (Oxford, U.K.: Oxford University Press, 2012), 28–29.

50. Michael Anthony Sells, *Stations of Desire: Love Elegies from Ibn `Arabi and New Poems* (Jerusalem: Ibis Editions, 2000); Hasan Mas`ud, *Perfect Harmony: Sufi Poetry of Ibn `Arabi* (Boston: Shambhala, 2002).

51. `Umar Ibn Al-Farid: Sufi Verse, Saintly Life*, trans. Th. Emil Homerin, Classics of Western Spirituality (Mahwah, N.J.: Paulist Press, 2001).

52. `Ali Ibn `Abdallah al-Shushtari, *Songs of Love and Devotion*, trans. Lourdes María Alvarez (Mahwah, N.J.: Paulist Press, 2010).

53. M. M. Badawi, "`Abbasid Poetry and Its Antecedents," in *`Abbasid Belles-Lettres*, 152–54.

54. Stefan Sperl discusses the *qasida* characteristics of a poem by Hallaj (number 75 in this collection) in "Qasida Form and Mystic Path in Thirteenth Century Egypt: A Poem by Ibn Al-Farid," in *Qasida Poetry in Islamic Asia and Africa*, ed. Stefan Sperl and Christopher Shackle (Leiden: Brill, 1996), 1:69–70.

55. For more on this topic see Diyab Qadid, "Malamih al-Sufiyya fi shi`r al-Mutanabbi" [Features of Sufism in the Poetry of al-Mutanabbi], *al-Ma`arij* 48–49 (2004), 265–97.

56. Homerin, "Tangled Words," 193; see also 194–96 on Mutanabbi.

57. Schimmel, *As through a Veil*, 21.

58. Farid al-Din `Attar Nishapuri, *Tadhkirat al-awliya'*, ed. Muhammad Isti`lami (1370; Tehran: Intisharat-i Zawwar, 1992), 490.

59. Carl W. Ernst, "Mystical Language and the Teaching Context in the Early Sufi Lexicons," in *Mysticism and Language*, ed. Steven T. Katz (Oxford, U.K.: Oxford University Press, 1992), 181–201.

60. *Kitáb al-Luma`*, 334.

61. Lings, "Mystical Poetry," 235–37.

62. Th. Emil Homerin, *Passion Before Me, My Fate Behind: Ibn Al-Farid and the Poetry of Recollection* (Albany: State University of New York Press, 2011), vii.

63. Hafiz, *Divan*, no. 143, accessed June 27, 2017, https://ganjoor.net/hafez/ghazal /sh143/.

64. *Kitáb al-Luma`*, 305.

65. Carl W. Ernst, "Wakened by the Dove's Trill: Structure and Meaning in the Arabic Preface of Rumi's *Mathnawi*, Book IV," in *The Philosophy of Ecstasy: Rumi and the Sufi Tradition*, ed. Leonard Lewisohn (London: I. B. Tauris, 2014), 259–68.

66. *Kitáb al-Luma`*, 232–33.

67. *Kitáb al-Luma`*, 234–35.

68. Muhammad Zayid, *Adabiyyat al-nass al-sufi bayn al-iblagh al-naf`i wal-ibda` al-fanni* [Literature of the Sufi text between practical expression and artistic creativity] (Irbid: Maktab al-Kitab al-Hadith, 2011), 125.

69. *Kitáb al-Luma`*, 249.

70. *Kitáb al-Luma`*, 299.

71. Homerin, "A Distant Fire."

72. Geert Jan van Gelder, "Rabi`a's Poem on the Two Kinds of Love: A Mystification?," in *Verse and the Fair Sex: Studies in Arabic Poetry and the Representation of Women in Arabic Literature: A Collection of Papers Presented at the 15th Congress of the Union Européenne Des Arabisants et Islamisants (Utrecht/Driebergen, September 13–19, 1990)*, ed. Frederick De Jong (Utrecht: M. Th. Houtsma Stichting, 1993), 66–75.

73. *Kitáb al-Luma`*, 234. Curiously, Qushayri quotes Abu `Ali al-Rudhbari as being deeply disapproving of a man who liked listening to music (*Al-Qushayri's Epistle on Sufism*, trans. Knysh, 62).

74. *Kitáb al-Luma`*, 235–36.

75. *Kitáb al-Luma`*, 270–71. Variants on this story are repeated by Hujwiri (*Revealing the Mystery*, 399–400) and Sa`di; see *The Gulistan (Rose Garden) of Sa'di: Bilingual English and Persian Edition with Vocabulary*, trans. W. M. Thackston (Bethesda, Md.: Ibex Publishers, 2008), book 2, story 27.

76. Carl W. Ernst and Bruce B. Lawrence, *Sufi Martyrs of Love: The Chishti Order in South Asia and Beyond* (New York: Palgrave, 2003).

77. Vision, particularly the vision of the divine in forms, is the focus of Cyrus Zargar, *Sufi Aesthetics: Beauty, Love, and the Human Form in the Writings of Ibn `Arabi and `Iraqi* (Charleston: The University of South Carolina Press, 2011).

78. Abu `Abd al-Rahman al-Sulami, "Kitab al-sama`," *Majmu`a-i athar-i Abu `Abd al-Rahman al-Sulami*, ed. Nasrollah Pourjavady (1372; Tehran: Markaz-i Nashr-i Danishgahi, 1994), 2:15–16.

79. Carl W. Ernst, "Sufism and the Art of Penmanship according to Siraj al-Shirazi's *Tuhfat al-Muhibbin* (1454)," *Journal of the American Oriental Society* 129.3 (2009), 431–42, citing 441–42.

80. *Kitáb al-Luma`*, 257.

81. al-Husayn b. Mansur al-Hallay [sic], *Diván*, trans. Clara Janés and Milagros Nuin (Madrid: Ediciones del Oriente y del Mediterráneo, 2002), 14–15.

82. Annemarie Schimmel, *Mystical Dimensions of Islam* (Chapel Hill: The University of North Carolina Press, 1975), 33.

83. Homerin, "Tangled Words," 193.

84. Hujwiri quotes ninety-two lines of poetry in his *Kashf al-mahjub* (ninety-one in Arabic and one in Persian), only identifying the author in nine cases. See Muhammad Husayn Tasbihi, *Tahlil-i kashf al-mahjub* (Lahore: Punjab University, 1999), 412.

85. *Kitáb al-Luma`*, 246–57.

86. Khargushi, *Tahdhib al-asrar fi usul al-tasawwuf*, 457–74.

87. Abu al-Hasan `Ali ibn al-Hasan al-Sirjani, *Al-Bayad wal-sawad min khasa'is hikam al-`ibad fi na`t al-murid wal-murad*, ed. Muhsin Purmukhtar (Tehran: Mu'assasa-i Puzhuhishi-i Hikmat o Falsafa-i Iran, 1390/2011), 196–205.

88. Farid al-Din `Attar Nishaburi, *Mantiq al-tayr*, 3rd ed., ed. Muhammad Javid Mashkur (1347; Tehran: Kitabfurushi-yi Tehran, 1969), 288, line 6.

89. Carl W. Ernst, "On Losing One's Head: Hallajian Themes in Works Attributed to `Attar," in *`Attar and the Persian Sufi Tradition: The Art of Spiritual Flight*, ed. Leonard Lewisohn and Christopher Shackle (London: I. B. Tauris, 2006), 330–43.

90. Michael Frishkopf, "Authorship in Sufi Poetry," *Alif: Journal of Comparative Poetics*, 23 (2003), 78–108.

91. Hujwiri, *Revealing the Mystery*, trans. Nicholson, 2.

92. Hilary Kilpatrick, *Making the Great Book of Songs: Compilation and the Author's Craft in Abu l-Faraj al-Isbahani's "Kitab al-aghani,"* RoutledgeCurzon Studies in Arabic and Middle Eastern Literatures (London: RoutledgeCurzon, 2003).

93. Kalabadhi, *The Doctrine of Sufis*, trans. Arberry, where the index only identifies twenty-five of sixty references to Hallaj. The nickname Abu al-Mughith appears to be drawn from the divine name "the Intercessor" (*mughith*), audaciously bestowed on Hallaj by his Indian disciples; see Massignon, *Passion*, 1:99.

94. These three poems (Massignon's M66, Y5, and Q8 in his edition of the *Diwan*) are numbered 77, 87, and 114 in this translation. Muddying the waters somewhat, Massignon (ibid., 148) classified the other five poems quoted by Kalabadhi as "suspect," without offering any reason, a decision mostly rejected by later editors. Four of those five poems are translated here (nos. 49, 93, 94, and 115).

95. Abu Ibrahim Isma`il ibn Muhammad Mustamli Bukhari, *Sharh al-ta`arruf li-madhhab al-tasawwuf*, ed. Muhammad Rawshan, 5 vols. continuously paginated (Tehran: Intisharat-i Asatir, 1363), 126, 672, 739, 901, 962, 1249, 1439, and especially 284 and 1683 (where he explicitly states that Hallaj is meant by "one of the great ones").

96. Sirjani, *Al-Bayad wal-sawad min khasa'is hikam al-`ibad fi na`t al-murid wal-murad*, pp. 48, 89 (attributed to Ibn `Ata'), 180, 181 (attributed to Abu `Ali al-Mawsili), 192, 195, 223–24, 243, 315, 326, 359 (attributed to Abu al-Hadid al-Misri), corresponding to poems 65, 45, 6, 99, 43, 113, 78, 107, 22, 114, and 101 in this translation.

97. "`Arabiyya. Arabic language and literature, (II) Second-Century Literature, (i) Poetry," *Encyclopaedia of Islam*, 2nd. ed, ed. P. Bearman, Th. Bianquis, C. E. Bosworth, E. van Donzel, and W. P. Heinrichs, Brill Online, 2013, accessed July 30, 2013.

98. Husayn Mansur Hallaj, *Divan* (Bombay: Duttprasad Press, 1894–1895), available online at http://babel.hathitrust.org.libproxy.lib.unc.edu/cgi/=pt?id=njp.3210107650 4206;view=1up;seq=4; *Divan-i Mansur Hallaj, ba sharh-i mabsuti dar bara-i `ishq-i ilahi* (Tihran: Kitabkhanah-i Sana'i, 1964); *Divan-i Mansur Hallaj*, ed. Muhsin Puyan (Qazvin: Tah, 2005).

99. Ernst, *Words of Ecstasy*, 37.

100. Rajab Tawhidiyan, "Ta'thir-padhiri-i Kamal al-Din Husayn Khwarizmi az Hafiz" [The influence on Kamal al-Din Husayn Khwarizmi from Hafiz], *Adabiyat o Zabanha [Literature and Languages]* 68 (1389/2010), 56–61, citing p. 57.

101. Shaybi², 9.

102. Ibid., 10. Similarly, two decades later the Lebanese scholar `Abduh Wazin dedicated his edition of the *Diwan al-Hallaj* to "the two Hallajians," Louis Massignon and Kamil al-Shaybi.

103. The literature devoted to discussing the life and works of Louis Massignon is quite extensive; a useful guide is the website http://louismassignon.org/, accessed May 30, 2017.

104. Giulio Basetti-Sani, *Louis Massignon (1883–1962): Christian Ecumenist Prophet of Inter-religious Reconciliation* (Chicago: Franciscan Herald Press, 1974).

105. Jeffrey J. Kripal, *Roads of Excess, Palaces of Wisdom: Eroticism & Reflexivity in the Study of Mysticism* (Chicago: University of Chicago Press, 2001).

106. Edward W. Said, *Orientalism* (London: Penguin, 2003).

107. Daniel Massignon and Jean Lacouture, *Le voyage en Mésopotamie et la conversion de Louis Massignon en 1908* (Paris: Editions du Cerf, 2001).

108. Louis Massignon, *Quatre textes inédits, relatifs à la biographie d'Al Ḥosayn-Ibn Manṣoūr Al-Ḥallāj* (Paris: Geuthner, 1914); Louis Massignon, ed., *Recueil de textes inédits concernant l'histoire de la mystique en pays d'Islam* (Paris: Guethner, 1929); al-Husayn ibn Mansur Hallaj, *Kitab al-Tawasin*, ed. Louis Massignon (Paris: P. Geuthner, 1913); Louis Massignon, ed., *Akhbār al-Ḥallāj: Recueil d'oraisons et d'exhortations du martyr mystique de L'islam Ḥusayn Ibn Manṣūr Ḥallāj* (Paris: Vrin, 1975); Louis Massignon, *Essay on the Origins of the Technical Language of Islamic Mysticism*, trans. Benjamin Clark (Notre Dame, Ind.: University of Notre Dame Press, 1997).

109. Herbert Mason, *Memoir of a Friend, Louis Massignon* (Notre Dame, Ind.: University of Notre Dame Press, 1988).

110. Massignon, *Passion*, 1:xxxix.

111. Ibid., 1:lxviii.

112. Ibid., 1:36–51.

113. Ibid., 2:5–9.

114. Ibid., 1:lv.

115. Ibid., 2:5.

116. Ibid., 2:116–17.

117. Ibid., 3:245–66.

118. Ibid., 3:245.

119. Ibid., 3:265.

120. Louis Massignon, ed., "Le *Dîwân* d'ál-Hallâj: Essai de reconstitution, édition, et traduction," *Journal Asiatique* (Janvier-Mars 1931), 1–158, quoting p. 7; henceforth cited as Massignon[1].

121. Ibid., 1.

122. Massignon, *Quatre textes inédits*, 51*–86* (these asterisks indicate pagination of the Arabic texts).

123. Massignon[1], 2, 8.

124. Ibid., 8.

125. Wendy deSouza, "Hostility and Hospitality: Muhammad Qazvini's Critique of Louis Massignon," *British Journal of Middle Eastern Studies* 40 (2013): 378–91; Hasan Hanafi and Zainab M. al-Hudayri, eds., *Fi qalb al-sharq: qira'a mu`asira li-a`mal Luwis Masīnyun* [*In the heart of the Orient: A contemporary reading of the works of Louis Massignon*] (Cairo: al-Majlis al-A`la lil-Thaqafa, 2003); Ali Badr, *Masinyun fi Baghdad: min al-ihtida al-sufi ilá al-hidayah al-kuluniyaliyah* [*Massignon in Baghdad: From Sufi quest to colonial guidance*], 2nd ed. (Beirut: al-Mu'assasa al-`Arabiyya lil-darasat wal-nashr, 2010).

126. `Abduh Wazin, ed. *Diwan al-Hallaj* (Bayrut: Dar al-Jadid, 1998), 13, citing Muhammad Jalal Sharaf.

127. Arab singers who have performed poems by Hallaj include Bashar Zarkan (Syria), Kazem al-Saher (Iraq), Jahida Wehbe (Lebanon), Yasin al-Tahami (Egypt), Dhafer Youssef (Tunisia), Abed Azrie (Syria), Marcel Khalifah (Lebanon), and Amina Alaoui (Morocco).

128. Issa Boulos describes his 2008 album *Hallaj* (UPC 877319003042) at http://issaboulos.com/hallaj.htm, accessed June 21, 2017.

129. Salah `Abd al-Sabur, *Murder in Baghdad (Ma'sat Hallaj), A Verse Play in Two Acts*, trans. Khalil I. Semaan, Arabic Translation Series of the *Journal of Arabic Literature*, 1 (Leiden: E. J. Brill, 1972).

130. Claudia Keilig, *Die Gestalt des irakischen Mystikers al-Hallaj im arabischen Theaterdrama: mit einer deutschen Übersetzung des Theaterstückes "Rihlat al-Hallaj" des tunesischen Dramatikers 'Izz ad-Din al-Madani* (Saarbrücken: VDM Verlag Dr. Müller, 2008).

131. See http://moderntimesstage.com/portfolio-item/hallaj-2011/, accessed December 22, 2017.

132. Khalil I. Semaan, "'Al-Hallāj,' A Poem by ʿAbd al-Wahhāb al-Bayātī," *Journal of Arabic Literature*, 10 (1979); 65–69; Reuven Snir, "A Study of 'Elegy for al-Hallāj' by Adūnīs," *Journal of Arabic Literature* 25, no. 3 (Nov. 1994): 245–56; Reuven Snir, *Religion, Mysticism and Modern Arabic Literature* (Wiesbaden: Harrassowitz, 2006), 81–90.

133. Ziad Elmarsafy, *Sufism in the Contemporary Arabic Novel* (Edinburgh: Edinburgh University Press, 2012).

134. Kamil Mustafa al-Shaybi, *Al-Hallaj mawduʿan lil-adab wal-funun al-ʿarabiyya wal-sharqiyya* [*Al-Hallaj as a literary and artistic subject in Arabic and Oriental literature*] (Baghdad: Matbaʿat al-Maʿarif, 1976), 342–51.

135. Ibid., 354–64.

136. "Kakayi—Tribute to Al-Hallaj," http://kakayi.webs.com/apps/videos/videos/show/13135394, accessed July 30, 2013.

137. Erol Akyavaş's *Istanbul Modern* exhibit is described at http://www.istanbulmodern.org/en/exhibitions/current-exhibitions/erol-akyavas-retrospective_1170.html, accessed July 3, 2013. I am grateful to Professor Recep Alpyagil of Istanbul University for drawing my attention to the work of Akyavaş.

138. "Erol Akyavaş work nets record amount at auction," *Hürriyet Daily News*, March 27, 2012, accessed July 30, 2013, http://www.hurriyetdailynews.com/Default.aspx?pageID=238&nid=16915.

139. For information about the exhibit *Amar Dawod: Al-Hallaj and The Tawasin* (December 2, 2013 – January 20, 2014), see http://meemartgallery.com/exhibitions_details.php?id=37.

140. This icon is available for sale on the website of Father Bill McNichols, referring to Louis Massignon's *Passion of Hallaj*; see https://fineartamerica.com/featured/islamic-mystic-and-martyr-al-hallaj-127-william-hart-mcnichols.html, accessed December 22, 2017.

141. R. M. A. Allen, "Arabic Poetry," in *The Princeton Encyclopedia of Poetry and Poetics*, ed. Stephen Cushman, Clare Cavanagh, and Paul Rouzer (Princeton, N.J.: Princeton University Press, 2012), 70.

POEMS

I.
Conventional
Love Lyrics

A number of poems attributed to Hallaj are basically conventional love po-
ems, with all the characteristics of court poetry and no overt indication of
any mystical interpretation. This does not exclude the possibility that such
poems may have circulated in Sufi circles and been read with additional
layers of meaning. One of these poems (no. 8) currently enjoys popularity
on the internet as a devotional address to the Prophet Muhammad. Never-
theless, these poems are characterized by a number of stereotyped features
that are familiar to the point of being clichés, including a use of hyperbole
and antithesis that is sometimes stretched to the limit. Exaggerated claims
of love's suffering are widespread in this section, and most of these verses
could be recited with a conventional love interpretation. For this reason, in
terms of content and vocabulary these poems may be considered conven-
tional love lyrics.

1. The Ardent Renouncer

Here a lover complains of the distance separating him from his remote beloved. At the same time, he begs a favor, while ironically claiming to be a lover who has renounced desire.

> It's sad enough that I call to you persistently
> > as though I were distant, or you were hidden.
> But I'm asking you a favor, without desire,
> > and I've seen none like me renouncing, while desiring.

2. Gathering Desire after Separation

This poem features paradoxical boasts about the intensity of love and the suffering that it causes. The hyperbole of these claims is muted by the balanced reversals of metaphors, and the complaint of persecution bolsters the lover's pleading.

> My heart had conflicting desires,
>> but my desires focused when my eye saw you.
> Everyone whom I envied, envied me,
>> but I became lord of all when you became my love.
> I left to the people their world and their religion,
>> absorbed in your love, oh my religion and my world!
> Friends and enemies only tease me about you
>> from ignorance of how much I'm suffering.
> 5   You lit two fires within me,
>> one in my ribs and the other in my guts.
> And I have never turned to quench my thirst
>> Without seeing your reflection in the water.
> That fire cools my heart like ice,
>> and a sword blow is softer than separation from my love.

3. Strengthen Me from the Sickness

This poem invokes the theme of the glance as the cause of falling in love and repeats a commonplace motif found in the work of Abu Nuwas and other poets: love is a disease for which it is also the cure.

> My gaze was the start of my disease.
>> Ah! My heart and what it committed!
> You who strengthen my sickness,
>> strengthen me from the sickness!

4. Dialogue of the Heart with the Truth

The first four lines occur in Hallaj's prose work, the *Tawasin* (5:11–12), in a passage immediately following a quotation from Qur'an 53:8—"he drew near and came down"—alluding to the Prophet Muhammad's ascension to paradise. Hallaj further comments, "He drew near in sublimity and came down in height, he drew near in desire and came down in joy." So this poem (and its eight-line expansion, marked off by a line of asterisks) could be seen as a mystical reenactment of that prophetic moment of ascension, enhanced by metaphysical use of "where" as a noun and Sufi concepts of annihilation and eternity. At the same time, it is a lover's complaint in its overall format, while the concept of joy (*tarab*) evokes music and poetry.

> I saw my Lord with the eye of my heart,
>> and he said, "Who are you?" I said, "You."
> There's no "where" to ask where you are,
>> and there's no "where," from your point of view.
> You're the one who owns every "where,"
>> but there is no "where" left—so where are you?
> Imagination has no imagination of you,
>> so that it could imagine where you are.

* * *

> 5   You've owned proximity's limit, so that
>> "where" doesn't know where you are.
> In my eternity, and in my non-eternity,
>> and in my annihilation, you were found.
> In effacing my name and the trace of my body
>> I asked about myself, and I said, You.
> My conscience pointed toward you, until
>> I was annihilated from myself, and you remained.
> My heart's protector vanished from me,
>> I knew my conscience, and you were you.
> 10   You are my life, the secret of my heart;
>> wherever I was, it was you.
> I comprehended everything in knowledge,
>> and everything that I saw was you.
> So give me forgiveness, my God,
>> for I have no hope from you except for you.

5. First the Guest, Then the House

This poem is an ironic allusion to the prophetic hadith, "First the guest, then the house." Rather than being an injunction to hospitality, the poem takes as its subject the idea of the heart as the home that welcomes the secrets of the beloved. Ultimately it is a prayer for annihilation.

> You pacified my heart, which keeps your secrets inside.
>> Congratulations to the house, or rather to the guest!
> There's nothing in it but a secret that I learned,
>> so see with your eye whether there is a dweller in the house.
> In a night of separation, whether short or long,
>> hope is my trusted friend there, and my memory.
> For I am pleased if my destruction pleases you;
>> you're my slayer, and whenever you choose, I choose.

6. Alchemical Expressions

This short poem begins with the highly conventional gesture of calling on the wind to be an emissary to the beloved, who is the even more conventional gazelle. The author's love is a passionate thirst that cannot be slaked. But then things are strangely transformed, with a lover who is inside and takes liberties, but their spirits are intertwined in love.

> Wind's breeze, tell the gazelle
> > that drinking only increases my thirst.
> I have a lover whose love is inside of me,
> > and if he wants, he strolls across my face.
> His spirit is mine, my spirit is his.
> > If he wishes, I do, and if I wish, so does he.

7. The Sun of Hearts

This short poem is a simple but transparent evocation of the image of the sun as an image of the beloved.

> My lover's sun arose by night
>> and glowed without setting.
> The daytime sun sets by night
>> but the sun of hearts is never hidden.
> One who loves his lover flies to him
>> in longing, to meet the lover.

8. Religion of Lovers, and Religion of the People

This poem of uncertain origin opens with a formulaic structure repeated in the first four verses and closes with a conventional request for a consoling song, addressed to an imagined tribal singer. The final line, a defiance of blame, uses Qur'anic language (109:6) to claim love as a religion.

> By God, the sun neither rises nor sets
> > without your love being joined to my sighs.
> I have not sat apart to talk with people
> > without you being my tale for all those present.
> Nor have I mentioned you in sorrow or joy
> > without you in my heart among the whispers.
> Nor have I aimed to drink water from thirst
> > without seeing your image in the cup.
> 5 If I could have come to you, I would have gone to you,
> > crawling on my face or walking on my head.
> Boy of the tribe, if you would sing a song for me!
> > So sing, though it's painful from your hardened heart.
> What do I care how many people blame me for a fool?
> > My religion's mine, and their religion's theirs.

9. The Lover's Punishment

This poem relies on conventional imagery of the suffering lover—such as the repeated dramatic complaints of the first three verses, the arrow glances of verse 4, and the invocation of the heart (literally, the liver or *kabid*) in verses 5 and 6—to describe the impossible situation of love. The ending adds a tone of sentimentality.

> I'm the one whose soul urges him on
> > to his violent death, though he's suspended.
> I'm the one whose life amid his worries
> > cries out from loneliness, although he's drowned.
> I am saddened, punished, and upset;
> > my spirit flees from the shackle of its lover.
> How can I endure, when he has thrown at my heart
> > arrows that were hurled from his glances?
> 5 And if my heart suggested a weaning,
> > it would have melted from worries' heat, and burned.
> Then appeared, from what the conscience had concealed,
> > tears of a message that told of its secret.

10. The Cure of Love

Abraham declared, "I am sick" (Qur'an 37:89) when he wrestled with the attraction of idols. Similar complaints are often made by courtly lovers who seek relief from the oppression of the lover. Despite the touch of irony in the third verse, the lover seems strikingly content with his lot.

> I am sick and ailing,
>> so heal me with your cure.
> I spill out my breath of life
>> in ships upon your satisfaction's ocean.
> I'm a prisoner, so tell me,
>> when will be the liberation?
> Until my spirit departs,
>> none of your oppressions hurt me.
> 5 Blessed is the eye of the lover
>> to whom you confer your vision,
> So in heart and soul there isn't
>> room for anyone but you.

11. Snakebite

Here is a romantic reflection on the bittersweet moment when lovers part.

> Poison from the tongues of snakes
>   is sweeter than a farewell kiss.
> I said goodbye while tears flowed,
>   when the call came for separation,
> Until the moment when separation called,
>   and I took off my veil in love for you.

12. The Rule of Lovers

This is another exaltation of the extreme suffering of the lover.

> Desire decreed for him that he should not taste of sleep,
>   though he passed the night with bitterness he'd never dreamt of.
> He said to his eye, "Be generous with tears, so
>   if you weep a lot, fine, otherwise let's use blood!"
> Among desire's conditions is that the lover sees
>   that longing's misery is always sweeter than happiness.

13. Letter from the Depth of Spirit

This unusually lengthy poem (thirty-four verses), rejected by Massignon, nonetheless has a compelling density of expression that recommends it, cast in the form of a letter. The first fourteen verses express conventional similes of love poetry, including relentless hyperbole about tears, wakefulness, and skinniness (verses 3–6; the sixth line is partly illegible). The only mystical touches are the identification of the beloved as "the Truth" in verse 12 and the ringing invocation of the self in verse 1, repeated at verse 15, which signals a different level of reflection. The latter is accompanied by an oath of Hallajian proportions, calling on the community ("by the truth's truth of the faithful"). After a reproach to the beloved in verse 16, the poet turns to a plural audience in verses 17 to 23 and then moralizes (verses 24–29) on the nature of love. The closing section (verses 30–34) makes a dramatic shift to adoration of the feminine beloved, in the process satirizing the conventional love poetry ("the ruins," etc.) that was the original pretext of the poem.

> My letter comes—oh I!
> > from utter sickness and weakness,
> And from an urgent heart,
> > and from illness and pain,
> From constant tears
> > that flow and float ships,
> From eyelids raised
> > that never tasted slumber,
> 5 From a skinniness that urges me
> > obediently to total annihilation,
> From an inner . . .
> > . . .
> So quit blaming me, critic!
> > I've lost my repose.
> The tears of my eyes have stopped,
> > and my pleasure's become trouble.
> Once I sought refuge and hid,
> > and I have no homeland.
> 10 I've destroyed my lifeblood in him,

and my longing is a habit,
And when I went with him, my garment
    became a bridle for others.
You, the Truth! To whom draws near
    anyone who draws near—
What's wrong with me? I'm struck by sickness,
    from rejection and languor.
What's wrong with me? A tormenter hurts me,
    but I haven't hurt even a stone.
15   Why is this? Oh I!
    by the truth's truth of the faithful—
Give an answer to a madman,
    who disputes the sadness in you!
All of you, bring him union,
    by parting from the parting of peers,
And observe the pact by which
    he rains benefits upon us!
For your example, my friends,
    is gorgeous—no, beautiful!
20   Wish fulfillers! Do you not
    see my longing revealed?
His testimony is needed,
    my realities are clear.
He asked me what he asked from you,
    so I went to him without me.
I went to you, with you,
    and you all became my homeland.
How long shall I remain
    like a worshipper who's fearful?
25   So I do not blame my blamer,
    since there's no slackness in blaming.
For love's pact exists in distance,
    and pleasure's best is feeble.
I think of him as the ocean,
    though he's free from cruel salt.
Be a breeze upon desire,
    since he's hidden from desire,
And look, so you will see wonders,

baffled at the geniuses there.
30   He who is she is the one who
        has filled me with sadness.
Desire's pact has destroyed her,
        since there is no guarantor.
He observed the rights that she had,
        continually, in the ruins.
But she gave up on him,
        though there is no giving up in love.
I keep my eye on a temptress,
        an idol who acts beautifully.

14. Where Is Your Match?

These verses maintain an intense focus on the glance as an excuse to praise the beloved.

> Blessed the moment when one caught
> you with a glance or two;
> And saw your beauty every day
> even once or twice.
> Essence of every sweetness,
> you're beyond every fault and disgrace;
> You're the foremost one in beauty,
> so where is your match? Where?

II.
Mystical Love Poems

These poems differ from those in the previous section by offering more explicit references to the spiritual ideals of the Sufi community. Those indications include technical terms, references to the Qur'an, narrative contexts, and metaphors that are sometimes stretched nearly out of recognition. While in formal terms these poems are hard to distinguish from conventional ones, they nevertheless transcend ordinary categories in one way or another.

15. The Veil of Invocation

This short piece juxtaposes two technical terms from Sufi practice: *walah*, a ravishing experience of love so extreme that it destroys the intellect with madness; and *dhikr*, remembering or recollecting God by reciting the divine names attested in the Qur'an. The point is that the conscious practice of remembering God itself becomes an obstacle, to the degree that it interferes with immediate experience.

> You're the one who drives me mad; remembering didn't madden me—
> let my heart have no link to remembering!
> Remembering is but a means that hides you from my gaze
> when my thought adorns it with my reflection.

16. Give Back to Me My Heart

The first verse alludes to the poets condemned in the Qur'an as those who "wander in every valley" (26:224–25). This embrace of estrangement and isolation acknowledges the inadequacy of poetry.

> Since you have owned my heart,
>> I've wandered in every valley.
> Give back to me my heart,
>> for I am even deprived of my sleep.
> I am a lonely stranger;
>> by you my isolation lengthens.

17. Constant Presence

While this poem exhibits the style of a conventional love poem with its neat antitheses, it has psychological depth, and its invocation of key Sufi vocabulary terms (union and separation, presence and absence) triggers additional layers of meaning that appeal to a mystical interpretation.

> You hid, but you did not hide from my mind,
>> so my sadness was mixed with my happiness.
> And the union was joined with a separation,
>> and my presence took place within my absence.
> For you are in the depth of my absent concern,
>> more hidden than the imagination in my mind.
> You truly are my companion by day,
>> and after dark you are my evening friend.

18. The Soul's Punishment in the Body's Prison

The circumstances of this poem are provided in *News of Hallaj*, narrative 38, where an ascetic disciple relates, "I heard al-Hallaj in the market of Baghdad shouting, 'People of Islam, save me! He does not release me and my soul so I can delight in it, and He does not seize me from my soul so I can be saved from it, and this is a teasing that I cannot endure.' Then he recited [these verses]." This poem is introduced with the rhetoric of repetition, which Hallaj frequently employs to express the transcendent ("all of your all"). The heart's estrangement is expressed in the familiar metaphor of prison.

> I've gathered, with my all, all of your all, my holy one.
>> You strip away the veil from me as though you were inside me.
> I turn my heart to things that are not you, but I only see
>> my desolation is from that; in it you are my solace.
> So that's why I'm in life's prison, removed
>> from affection; so free me from this prison to you!

19. Lovers' Perfection

As narrated in *News of Hallaj* (no. 43), this poem was a rueful comment by Hallaj after a long night of praying and reciting the Qur'an, in which he criticized himself for thinking that he could please God by prayer. This is a criticism of the Sufi practice of remembrance (*dhikr*) when the ego obscures the object of memory—that is, God.

> When a youth reaches perfection from desire,
>> and loses the remembered one in memory's pride,
> he witnesses truth when desire attests to him
>> that lovers' perfection is infidelity.

20. Nearness and Distance Are One

In Hallaj's *Tawasin* (6:12), these verses summarize the defiant attitude of the Islamic Satan, Iblis, after he defended himself for refusing to bow down before Adam as God commanded in the Qur'an (7:12). Iblis's argument was that he was superior to Adam in his service and love of God, for he was the true monotheist. This is a tangled poem, playing on the terms "distance" (*bu`d*) and "nearness" (*qurb*), commonly used in Sufi language to define the relationship to God.

> I have no distance, after your distance, after
>> I became certain that nearness and distance are one.
> Even if I am exiled, exile is my companion—
>> but how is exile right when love is found?
> Yours is the praise, with all success, with all purity,
>> for a clever worshipper who bows to none but you.

21. Transcendence

The first three verses of this poem are recited in *News of Hallaj*, narrative 12, as he dictates to his students a negative theology, describing God as beyond all rational categories. These verses, which contain a detour into love poetry, capture Hallaj's despair at the limitations of reason. The last verse alludes to the divine manifestation in humanity and the refusal of Iblis to recognize it.

> My denial sanctifies you;
>> my thought of you is confusing.
> A love has astonished me,
>> and a glance that's arched.
> And the proof of love has shown
>> that nearness is a deception,
> For Adam is nothing but you
>> And Iblis is in the middle.

22. The Promise of Love

This poem depicts an inner relationship of great intensity, one that evades the scrutiny of consciousness. It can be seen as a reflection on the speech of God in the Qur'an, a meditation on the archetypal words that remain beyond perception. Here Hallaj plays with the divine essence and attributes like a preoccupied lover.

> I have a friend who visits when no one's around.
>> He's present, but he's gone when I am looking.
> You won't see me listening to him closely,
>> so I can be aware of words he's saying,
> Words without letters or punctuation,
>> unlike the pronunciation of sounds.
> It's as though I'm speaking to him
>> of my thoughts, by myself, to myself.
> 5   Present, absent, near, or far, he's
>> someone customary qualities don't contain.
> He is nearer than my conscience to my thought,
>> and more hidden than the glimpse of inspirations.

23. Removing the Veil

This poem is a demonstration of affectionate exaggeration taken to an extreme.

> You are the sun, the moon, and the day!
> > You are our paradise and our hellfire.
> Avoiding sin with you is but a sin,
> > and fear of nakedness is nakedness.
> People throw off all restraint with you—
> > so what of one with no restraint at all?

24. Voyager of Desire

Here is a vivid metaphorical portrayal of desire as an ocean, culminating in panic and a lover's anxious complaint.

> I keep floating on seas of desire;
>> the wave lifts me up, then I go down.
> As much as its wave lifts me up
>> I fall and then I plunge inside,
> Until He carries me by love,
>> to a place that has no shore.
> I called out, "You whose name I can't disclose!"
>> —nor do I betray him ever in love—
> "My soul fears you as an unjust judge;
>> this was not the deal we had between us!"

25. While Love Remains Secret

This poem is a celebration of making love public and taking the consequences, since the risk is all the more exciting. It ends with a vow never to give up when discovered.

> While love remains secret, it's dangerous,
>> and ultimate safety means to lower one's guard.
> The most beautiful love is the one that gossip betrays,
>> just as fire is useless when it remains in the stone.
> When the jailer appears, and the guards collect,
>> and the informer writes down my name,
> I hope my soul would disown my love for you
>> only after I disown my eyes and my ears!

26. Veil of the Heart

This poem is a meditation on the ego as the unavoidable shadow that prevents the discovery of the secret of love.

A secret appeared to you, but you were slow to discover it.
A dawn appeared, but you were its shadow.
For you are the veil of the heart from its hidden secret.
If it weren't for you, its seal would not have been stamped.

27. Eyes of the Heart

While Massignon saw in this short poem a reference to the theology of extreme Shiʿism ("meaning," as an allusion to God), a more convincing reading comes from the Sufi theorist Ibn Dabbagh, who sees here the spiritual lover hidden from the public. This love is a mutual recognition that God establishes between two hearts, which no one else is aware of.

> In you is a meaning that calls souls to you,
>> and a proof that demonstrates you by yourself.
> I have a heart with eyes
>> gazing at you, and all of it belongs to you.

28. Burden of the Heart

While this verse can be taken to describe the sufferings of an ordinary lover, it has been used as a comment on the Qur'anic story (33:72) of the burden of responsibility that God gave humanity when the rest of creation avoided it.

> You have caused the heart to bear what the body does not bear,
>   for the heart bears what the body does not bear.
> Would that I were the closest of those who seek your aid,
>   with an eye to see you, or would that I had an ear.

29. Prison Letter

According to *News of Hallaj* (no. *2), Hallaj wrote these lines on a letter from prison to his friend Ibn ʿAtaʾ, after he had sealed it. While the poem is addressed to God, it testifies to the close relationship between the two Sufis.

> My concern for him is passion for you—
>> you, toward whom our allusions point!
> We are two spirits joined by longing
>> in what touches you, and in your presence.

30. In All Directions

This poem is a close observation of self, starting with the eyes (watchers) and ears (witnesses), beginning in the third person but then shifting to direct address. It is an oath of undivided love.

> I have two watchers who witness that he loves me—
> and for me there are two witnesses that you see me.
> No thought occurs in my conscience of anyone but you,
> and my tongue speaks only of your desire.
> So if I sought the east, in the east you would be its east,
> and if I sought the west, you would be right in front of me.
> And if I sought above, then above it, you would be above,
> and if I sought below, you are every place.
> 5   And you are where the all is—rather, you are nowhere!
> You are all in all without ever fading,
> In my heart, my spirit, my mind, my thought,
> my repeated breaths, and the bond of my tongue!

31. Something by My Heart

Here the poet speaks of the heart as the repository of the divine names. In both the first and last verses, he proclaims the heart as a mystery that remains opaque even to cosmic entities (the tablet and the pen are familiar Near Eastern symbols of the decree of destiny and the intellectual principle).

> There is something by my heart, and in it are names from you.
>> Light doesn't know it, not at all, nor darkness.
> And the light of your face is a secret, when I witness it.
>> This is generosity, virtue, and nobility.
> So take my story, my love, for you know it;
>> the Tablet doesn't know it, in truth, nor the Pen!

32. Speech from the Beloved

This poem concisely deploys a highly experiential language to claim an exalted, nearly prophetic status for the poet. It occurs in the *Tawasin* (3:11), immediately after Hallaj compares himself to the burning bush encountered by Moses.

> The Truth spoke to me from my heart,
>> and my knowledge was upon my tongue.
> He drew me near to him after I was distant,
>> and God chose me, and selected me.

33. Hidden, Present

This poem presents the opposition between the realms of the hidden (*ghayb*) and the visible (*shahada*). The paradox is that the absent one is present through that absence. The seeming resolution by nearness in the third verse fails to explain the absence. Who is it that speaks and witnesses?

> You, hidden, present, in the moment of his hiding—
>> if your person hides, the reminder still exists.
> Giving you up leads to unfortunate results,
>> but abstaining from other things is to be praised!
> Whoever nears you reaches all the good,
>> but one who leaves you is grieving and heartsick.

34. I Wonder at You and Me

Massignon classified this poem as a *qasida*, despite its brevity. It closely follows a single idea, the poet's total identification with the beloved. Yet the final line echoes key terms from the first verse (the insistent repetition of "wish"), recalling the symmetrical structure found in the *qasida*. Some Sufis considered this poem evidence that Hallaj was stuck at the beginning stage of annihilation (*fana'*), wrongly thinking himself to be identical with his beloved.

> I wonder at you and me—
>   you're the wish I wished for!
> You drew me near, so close
>   I thought you were me.
> And I was lost in ecstasy, until
>   you annihilated me from my self, by your self.
> You are my ease in my life,
>   and my peace after I'm buried.
> 5 I have no intimate but you,
>   whether you are my fear or my safety.
> The gardens of your meanings
>   contain every art!
> And if I wish for anything,
>   you are all that I wish.

35. I Found You by Sciences

This poem plays on the well-known ambiguity contained in the Arabic root W-J-D, which has the basic physical meaning of "finding" but also, in Sufi circles, carries the connotation of "ecstasy" (*wajd*). The paradox here is that the poet claims to experience the infinite God through reason and external appearance—a claim that is ironically questioned. At the same time, one can seek God through hidden mysteries, but their inner secret is inadequate without the external. Divine love remains hard to comprehend.

> I found you by sciences and their ecstasy.
>> Who has found you without sciences of appearance!
> I found you by mysteries and their secret,
>> and there in you was the secret—the one that's useless.
> I am amazed at a worthy one who knows
>> your subtle love, how he fails to reflect.

36. Open Secret

Here is advice to lovers, from one who knows better.

> You who walk around love's door from passion
>> and hide love, even though it's an open secret,
> Look at his face—not the face of his form—
>> when he shows himself to lovers and friends,
> And tell him, without shame, "Hello! You are me—
>> your description erased the proof of my qualities!"

37. Loss in Ecstasy Is Loss

This poem lays out the role of the lover with brevity and irony, stressing the gap between thought and reality. The surprise is the way that the lover gets taken for the beloved, becoming a master through servitude.

> Thinking ecstasy is ecstasy;
> > loss in ecstasy is loss.
> Distance for me is near to you;
> > nearness for me is far from you.
> How can one prove a second
> > when you, unique one, are unique?
> So that is the heart for meanings,
> > and of that there is no doubt.
> Idolatry proves an other,
> > though it surely is a struggle.
> From that, it so happens that I
> > in an other's form am counted.
> People count me for a master
> > just because I am his servant.

5

38. I Didn't Long

This brief piece moves from intoxication to longing and ultimately knowledge.

> I didn't long to attain him except if I was caught
> > by staggering drunkenness in the midst of astonishment,
> Until, when those who gaze at him left me,
> > I found myself a knower, and the essence was laid out before me.

III.
Martyrdom

This section is characterized by poems that unmistakably refer to the unavoidable death and annihilation of the lover, an insistent reminder of Hallaj's execution. It is not clear whether these are prophecies or retroactive figurations. They contain some of the most memorable images in Hallaj's poetry, particularly the famous "Kill Me, Friends" (no. 44). Whether all of these were written by Hallaj or not, they are reminders of the way his career itself became a metaphor for Sufi concepts.

39. Testament

This poem is a dramatic embrace of martyrdom, enhanced by its calm announcement to the community of friends, the Sufis. The notorious second verse, with its clear allusion to the crucifixion of Jesus, has occasioned some comment. Abu al-`Abbas al-Mursi, the celebrated North African Sufi, is quoted as saying, "I abhor two characteristics of the jurists: their opinion that Hallaj was an infidel, and their opinion that al-Khidr is dead. But it is not established that al-Hallaj deserved to be killed, and the correct interpretation of his saying, 'My death will be upon the faith of the cross,' means that he will die upon the faith of his self [`ala dini nafsihi], because he was crucified." This poem is included in *News of Hallaj* (no. 52) as his prophecy of his own martyrdom. This narrative suggests that the poet deliberately chose language that would cause a strong negative reaction.

> Hey there! Inform my friends that I
>> have gone to sea and my ship is wrecked!
> My death will be in the faith of the cross,
>> and I want neither Mecca nor Medina.

40. All of Me Becomes a Heart

Here is an intense meditation on love as suffering.

When I recall you, longing almost kills me,
    but forgetting you is sorrows and pains.
All of me becomes a heart calling to you,
    for suffering and hastening the agonies.

41. Blameless

This poem is the complaint of Iblis, quoted in the *Tawasin* (6:29). It occurs immediately after the following dialogue between Iblis and God (6:28), in which Iblis defends himself for refusing to prostrate before Adam:

> God most high said to him, "The choice is mine, not yours." He replied, "All choices are yours, and my choice is yours, which I have chosen for myself, oh wonder! And even if you prevented me from prostrating to him, then you are the Preventer; and if I am mistaken in my words, do not exile me, for you are the Listener; and if you wanted me to prostrate to him, then I am the Obedient. I do not know of any of the knowers who knows you better than me."

Whether Hallaj accepted this argument or simply reported it in provocation is a matter of debate, though the parallel between Iblis and Hallaj is hard to ignore.

> Don't blame me, for blame is far from me.
>> Save me, my lord, because I am alone.
> I am true to your true promise;
>> in the beginning, my affair was hard from the start.
> Whoever wants speech, here's my writing,
>> so read it, and know I am a martyr.

42. Dyed in Blood

The shocking image of a bloody finger also evokes the bridal adornment with henna. So in addition to depicting the fate of God's lovers, this verse, on another level, warns against attacking those (the Sufis) who are decorated like God's brides.

> Don't mince words with us, for here is a finger
> that we have dyed with the blood of lovers.

43. My Drinking Buddy

While some have pictured Hallaj addressing this poem ecstatically to God during his execution (see *News of Hallaj*, no. 16), others have seen it as a profane poem, ascribed to Abu Nuwas or al-Husayn ibn al-Dahhak, on the fate of those who associate too closely with corrupt kings. In either case it concerns the capriciousness of absolute rulers toward their boon companions; the "mat" was part of the executioner's equipment for decapitation, a bad sign for a guest.

> My drinking buddy's not accused
>   of anything unjust.
> He pours for me the stuff he drinks,
>   in the way of host and guest.
> But then he called for the sword and mat
>   when the cup had circled past.
> So fares the drinker of pure wine,
>   while summer's dog days last.

44. Kill Me, Friends

In this three-part ode (the division into parts is marked by rows of aster-
isks), Hallaj begins by addressing his friends the Sufis by calling for his own
execution. Using bold theological language, he demands the erasure of his
essence (*dhat*) and laments the persistence of his attributes (*sifat*). Repeat-
ing the command to kill him, he foresees his friends passing by the traces
of his grave, evoking the typical opening scenario of the classical Arabic
ode. A true lover, we are told, keeps his love secret to the grave—an ironic
observation for Hallaj, who told his secret to all.

The second part is a riddle about overcoming time, told in the first
person and filled with paradoxes and reversals. Hallaj returns to live in the
grave that previously contained his dust. This is the enigma of resurrection
and immortality.

In the third part, he turns to a single close friend, repeatedly command-
ing him to assemble his scattered remains from the four elements and plant
them. The result is a miraculous flower that blooms, thanks to the sevenfold
libation that his friend pours over his remains. With its description of a
transformation of the self that takes place on a cosmic scale, this poem has
some of the typical qualities of a *qasida*, complete with a striking wordplay
in the next-to-last line.

> Kill me, friends,
>   for in my killing is my life.
> My death is in my life;
>   my life is in my death.
> Annihilation of my essence
>   is the noblest of my glories.
> And my attributes remaining
>   is the foulest of my crimes.
> 5   My spirit tires of my life
>   amid its lingering traces,
> So kill me, burn me
>   in these fading bones,
> And later pass my dust
>   in ruined tombs—
> You will find my lover's secret
>   folded into my remains.

I was a mighty patriarch
    of lofty rank,
10 Then I became a child
    in wet nurses' chambers,
Living in a grave's niche,
    in marshy grounds.
My mother bore her father—
    that's one of my marvels—
Then my daughters, after they were
    daughters, were my sisters.
This was no deed of time,
    nor act of adultery.

***

15 So gather all my parts together
    from burning bodies,
From air and fire,
    and next from water pure,
Then plant it all in earth
    whose soil is fallow,
And swear to water it
    from cups passed round
By running waitresses
    with running waters—
20 When you finish seven,
    the best of plants will bloom.

45. Punishment

This poem does not need to be taken literally as a masochistic expression. Instead, it is a simple but clear inversion of the common fatuous declarations of love.

> I want you, but I don't want you for a reward—
>   I want you, instead, for the penalty.
> And all of my desires I have attained
>   except the delight of finding myself punished.

46. Sacrifice

This poem is a powerful reflection that hinges on the analogy between suffering for love and the Abrahamic sacrifice of animals at the hajj. It still takes the form of a lover's complaint, with the customary defiance of blame. The spiritualization of the hajj and its sacrifice would indeed play a crucial role in Hallaj's trial and execution.

> The lover who's pleased to sacrifice me
>> sees it as lawful, whether they let him or not.
> Even if shedding my blood was the least of your desires,
>> your glance never flinched from my sacrifice.
> God! If my spirit knew who it's joined to,
>> it would stand on its head instead of its feet.
> Critic, don't blame my longing for him, for if
>> you saw him as I do, you would not blame.
> 5   There are some who circle the Ka`ba without the use of limbs;
>> if they circled God, they'd no longer need the shrine.
> The beloved slaughters a soul on the day of their feast,
>> while the people slaughter the likes of sheep and goats.
> The people have their pilgrimage, but I have a pilgrimage to my rest.
>> Their offerings are animals, while my heart and blood are offered.

47. Infidel

This striking couplet occurs in *News of Hallaj* (no. 66) in the context of an unusual story in which Hallaj asks a friend to feed a dog, which he describes as his now-tamed carnal soul. In his happiness at this victory over the ego, he announces in this verse his desire for martyrdom, a notable example of an ecstatic saying (*shath*) that is outwardly repugnant but inwardly sublime.

> I rejected the religion of God; infidelity is my duty,
>   because it is detestable to Muslims.

48. The Fate of the Arrogant

Here is a concise reflection on love and arrogance.

I was arrogant in the fortune of desire,
    and the fate of the arrogant caught me.

49. You've Watched Me

While this poem begins by thanking the beloved for protection, it shifts into a portrait of the Sufi who ascends, like the Prophet Muhammad, to the divine presence, and who then returns bearing pearls from the divine ocean for the benefit of others. Yet the annihilation he has suffered makes him a martyr, who lives despite his death.

> You've watched me protectively so that
>   I was saved from a place of plague.
> For you are my pretext in these debates,
>   and in my thirst you quench me.
> And when the mystic climbs to the temple,
>   he goes by night to a lofty vantage place
> and dives into abundant oceans
>   that overflow with thought of revelation.
> 5 He breaks the seal of hidden things to get
>   what brings to life the heart of the troubled friend.
> He's astounded from the shock of the meeting—
>   you'll think him dead, although he is alive.

50. The Thread of Desire

This simple quatrain plays on the symbolism of weaving and wool carding associated with the name of Hallaj (literally, "the wool carder") while predicting his martyrdom.

> I will gather the thread of desire into a ball
> and weave for people with every art.
> And I will water the plants of desire with my tears,
> for I have drunk from the cup of persecutions.

IV.
Metaphysics

This is an extensive group of poems that engage with the technical terms and metaphysical concepts of Sufism. Some of them have an experiential flavor, as the author struggles with the inadequacy of words or feels overcome by prophetic messages. Speculations on the role of reason in understanding creation pervade these lines. How does rational reflection relate to ecstasy and the annihilation of self? The conclusive example is the evocation of cosmic love in poem 70, "Love Is in Primordial Eternity."

51. Cramped

A setting for this poem is furnished by *News of Hallaj*, narrative 11, in which the author announces to a crowd in the mosque that his experiences have exceeded the capacity of words to express them. These verses concisely convey the sense of a heart that cannot be contained by this world.

> I wonder at my all, how it bears a part of me,
>> when just from the weight of a part, my earth can't bear me.
> If there were a resting place on the breadth of earth,
>> my heart would still be cramped by the breadth of creation.

52. Illumination

This poem occurs in a dramatic episode of *News of Hallaj* (no. 10) in which Hallaj pleads with the people in a Baghdad bazaar and in a mosque, expressing in cryptic terms his overwhelming experience of God. The poem calls on Qur'anic images, including the light verse (24:35) and the apocalyptic last trumpet, and concludes with the revelation of Moses.

> The covenant of prophecy is a lamp of light
>> hung by revelation in the chamber of the heart.
> By God, he blows the spirit's breath into my mind,
>> into my thought—the breath of Israfil's last trumpet!
> When he appeared to my spirit, to speak with me,
>> I saw, in my rapture, Moses stand on Sinai.

53. God's Explanation

Here is another poem obsessing on the truth (*haqq*), a synonym for God, a term repeated here, either as indefinite or definite, a total of nine times. Truth is its own proof, beyond explanation.

> Explaining truth's explanation? You are the explanation!
>> And for every explanation, you are the tongue that tells it.
> I pointed to a truth with truth, but for everyone
>> who pointed to a truth, you are the guarantee.
> The truth of truth is astonished, even if truth is speaking,
>> so the tongue is silent, since its message has reached you.
> If the nature of truth was clear to the truth,
>> then why is its location hidden in the people?

54. Knower of the Revelation

This dense couplet starts with an apocalyptic question, demanding whether there is anyone who knows the revelation (*naba'*) as God does. This radiant interrogation is itself the manifestation of the seeker's goal; the question answers itself.

> The reality of Truth is radiating
> > a cry: "Does revelation have a knower?"
> Reality has already manifested;
> > difficult is the goal of one who seeks it.

55. Temple and Light

This poem presents an anthropology describing, first, the elemental and material human body, then the luminous spark that is divine.

> Body like a temple, luminous of heart,
>> spirit that's eternal, devout, wise,
> he returns with the spirit to its lords,
>> but the temple remains rotting in the dust.

56. Reason's Ears and Eyes

These verses accompany a report in *News of Hallaj* (no. 33) expanding on the notion that unity's essence is contained in successive levels of consciousness. The poem finds this kind of hierarchy in lights, secrets, existence, and even reason.

> For the lights of the light of lights, there are lights in creation,
>> and for the secret, in the secret of the secret ones, there are secrets.
> For existence in existents, there is a Giver of existence,
>> who is fond of my heart, and he guides and chooses.
> Consider with your reason's eye what I describe—
>> for reason, there are watchful ears and eyes.

57. How Often Were We Hidden

Massignon considers this poem "surely apocryphal" (Massignon[1], 36), noting that its only transmitter is al-Jawbari, a thirteenth-century author of an unusual history of frauds and impostors in Islamic civilization who describes these three verses as being part of a longer poem by Hallaj on the secret of invisibility. The second verse alludes to substances used by magicians in order to hide invisibly or to summon spirits. Al-Jawbari's attitude toward Hallaj is ambivalent; he places Hallaj at the very beginning of his chapter on fake Sufis but also recounts his martyrdom and quotes his poetry.

> How often were we hidden from the shapes of sight
>> by a dot whose brilliance resembles the moon?
> A dot of sesame, sesame oil, and letters,
>> and jasmine, that's been written on a forehead.
> Go, and we shall go, and we shall see your figures,
>> but you will not see us, you who are past.

58. Ecstasies and States

A framework for this poem is provided in *News of Hallaj* narrative 36, where a disciple describes how Hallaj with great emotion revealed to the people of Baghdad what happens to someone who encounters God directly, and then recited the poem. This anecdote helps explain the apparently unfinished form of the poem, which promises to explain three states of the soul but only mentions two. In the story, Hallaj relates three experiences: (1) being possessed by God and emptied of others; (2) being seized by God and annihilated; and (3) being attacked by God's worshippers so that one only seeks God. Since the first two of these experiences match up with the two states mentioned in the closing verses, the poem's abrupt ending may be seen as a silent gesture toward the third state, predicting the persecution of Hallaj as the logical outcome. The key concepts here are ecstasy (*wajd*), the initial "finding" of God, and the conscience (*sirr, sarira*), the faculty that apprehends the inner secret.

> God makes all the ecstasies of Truth's ecstatic states,
> > though great intellects fall short of these.
> And ecstasy is nothing but a thought, and then a glance,
> > drunk in flames beneath these consciences.
> When God lives in one's conscience, it replicates
> > three of the soul's states for the insightful:
> One state destroys the conscience from the depth of its description
> > but brings it back in ecstasy, in the state of one amazed.
> 5 A second state restrains conscience's heights, and faces
> > a view erasing it from every viewer. . . .

59. What Wonderful Relief

In this challenging poem, Hallaj evokes grace as a rainstorm on a mountain—
and where else could this scene be but on Mount Sinai? Lightning flashes
freeze repeated images of lover and beloved, like prophet and deity locked
in a glance. Community is distorted in the brothers whose vision is confused
by revelation, and in the waters that flow from the divine ocean. Ultimately
this is an encounter with reality, not the romantic figures of Bedouin camp-
sites. The poem closes ironically with the speaker rejecting the relief of the
opening, acting like a violent patient until overcome by vision.

> What wonderful relief is symbolized by hidden grace
>> from a lightning flash that glows within, above his clouds.
> Now he looks at me just so, and then I look at him;
>> if he wished, from his mountains he would veil my brothers.
> Now he looks toward him, and in him by his effort,
>> from the pouring ocean overflowing with his waters.
> For the All sees all of me, and I see him
>> with reality, not through his romantic character.
> 5   I erase his relief, until I start to see him,
>> like a man who yells at his diseases' healers.

60. Riding on Reality

Again playing with the word for the real/truth/God (*haqq*), this poem employs the image of riding to confront the riddle of existence.

> Riding on reality is real for God,
>> but the meaning of the expression is subtle here.
> I rode existence into nonexistence,
>> but it still didn't soften my hardened heart.

61. The Conscience and the Path

This poem, like poem 32, occurs in the *Tawasin* (3:11) just after Hallaj describes Moses's encounter with God in the burning bush; Hallaj explains that he himself is that bush. The implication is that, just as the words of the bush are God's, so are the words of Hallaj. "Reality is reality, and creation is creation; leave creation so you can become He, and He you, in relation to reality" (*Tawasin* 3:8). Transformation is accomplished here by means both transcendental and conventional. The *H* stands for *huwa*, "He," the divine identity.

> God turned me into the *H* of reality,
>> by promise, by contract, and by decree.
> My conscience witnesses, without awareness;
>> this one's my conscience, and that one's a path.

62. The Secret of Mysteries

This piece reflects on the nature of revelation, of which the simplest formulation is the Muslim profession of faith: the negation of the unreal ("there is no god") and the affirmation of the real ("but God"). And when the Qur'an provides seemingly anthropomorphic descriptions of God's face and hands, theologians accept them "without asking how." Nevertheless, an ignorant humanity remains content with mere allusions, unaware of God's presence within them.

> The secret of mysteries is wrapped in an affirmation
> > at the horizon's edge, in folds of light.
> But how? For the "how" is known externally,
> > while the hidden exists, inwardly, for and by the essence.
> Creatures stray in a blind darkness,
> > seeking, but they only know allusions.
> They think and imagine that their quest reaches truth;
> > facing the sky, they whisper prayers to the heavens.
> 5 The Lord is with them in every revolution,
> > dwelling in their states at every moment.
> If they only knew, they wouldn't leave him for an instant,
> > for he does not leave them at any moment.

63. I've Thought about Religions

These lines are quoted in *News of Hallaj* narrative 45, in which one of Hallaj's disciples relates an encounter in the market with a Jew, whom he insulted—a story that meets with Hallaj's displeasure, as he sees religions as decreed by God and sharing the same goal.

> I've thought about religions as a thorough investigator,
>   and I've found them to be a root with many branches.
> So don't demand that a man have one religion, since
>   he'll be turned away from the firm root. It's just
> the root that should seek him, to explain to him
>   all sublimities and meanings; then he'll understand.

64. Name and Meaning

This verse poses the question of the relation between name and meaning, since possession of the former encourages the delusion that one has also reached the latter. This attainment of knowledge, of deducing the cause of things, is only possible through God.

> A name joined with creatures—they wander round it, madly longing
> > that from it they'd learn just one of His meanings.
> By God, from this they'll never reach a cause
> > that would reveal the One who revealed it.

65. Near and Far

This poem sums up an episode in *News of Hallaj* narrative 51, in which a disciple asks Hallaj how he should seek God. Hallaj replies with his negative theology, concluding that "He is isolated from creatures by eternity as they are isolated from him by time. How is the path to be sought to the one who has this quality?" He wept as he delivered these lines, which end with muted irony.

> I said, "Dear friends, it's the sun; its light
>   is near!" But there is distance in its approach.

66. Intimacy with God

This poem conveys a sense of intimate identification with God, an overde-termination of meaning, that is also a mutual relationship based on divine omnipresence. This revelation is here disclosed to a community.

> His existence is through me, and my existence is through him.
>   As for his description, he's the one who tells it.
> If not for him, I'd know no guidance, and
>   if not for me, he'd have no knower!
> In every meaning there is something that means him,
>   so tell those who contradict me, "You are wrong!"
> There is nothing but the Merciful, my friends,
>   with which our spirits can be intimate.

67. Vanishing Ascension

This verse offers a neat demonstration of how to describe the vanishing of the ego.

> I went up so high that his existence vanished from me.
> Then I vanished from the ecstasy I found there.

68. I Have Control of Things

This philosophical reflection posits an idea that reminds one of a first cause or an unmoved mover, which is not a fancy of the imagination but the origin of all. This idea is introduced even as the author takes on the role of demiurge, to whom God has entrusted control of created things. The vocabulary and concept of this poem evoke the register of philosophy, depicting the role of the imam or saint who represents God's authority on earth.

> I have control of things that I do not know,
>> yet I'm not distinct from what I control.
> So an idea occurs to me that reminds me of a mover,
>> which is not a fancy concocted by imagination.

69. Consider My Apparition

This poem builds on an allusion to the Prophet Muhammad's vision of God in Qur'an 53:7, "while He was on the highest horizon." Hallaj audaciously proposes his own fanciful apparition as a rival to the prophetic vision of God (or, more conventionally, the vision of Gabriel). Yet, ironically, it is Hallaj who melts and vanishes, while the crescent moon grows. This seems to be a metaphor for his psychic annihilation during the process of revelation, from which he is now externalized.

> Consider my apparition and the crescent moon, when it appears
> to his vision on his horizon—which of us is brighter?
> Though it increases every hour,
> growing, while I melt and vanish in desire.

70. Love Is in Primordial Eternity

This extraordinary lyric poem is at once a declaration of love as the essence of God and a depiction of the community of lovers, comprising martyrs who go to their death—the great ones who are humbled. This poem is clearly connected to Hallaj's long prose passage on love as an essential attribute of God, preserved by Daylami in his tenth-century treatise on philosophical and mystical theories of love. The theological description of essence and attributes in pre-eternity is couched in tangled prepositions. The poem turns on the fifth verse, using the Arabic letters for L (*lam*) and A (*alif*), which had just repeatedly occurred in the fourth verse, "in him gleamed a shining" (*fa-la'la'a fihi la'la'u*). The two letters L and A thus typify the lover and the beloved, and the radiance that connects them is construed in later poetry as the smoldering glance or wink, the source of the burning passion of love.

> Love is in primordial eternity eternally,
>   in Him, by Him, from Him; it begins in Him.
> Love is not temporal, since it was an attribute,
>   an attribute of the One whose martyrs are alive.
> His attributes are from Him, in Him, but not temporal,
>   for temporality is what begins in things.
> When the beginning began, his love began as an attribute
>   in that which began—and in him gleamed a shining!
> For the L was affectionate with the inclined A—
>   and both were one, which means in the beginning.
> But in separation they are two; when they are together
>   separately, one's the devotee, and one's the Lord.
> These are the realities: the fire of longing, burning
>   for reality, whether they stay or go.
> They're humble, worthless, when they are mad with love,
>   for the mighty become humbled in their longing.

V.
Prayers and Sermons

These poems have either the formal characteristics of a direct address to the deity, as in prayer, or the rhetoric of moral persuasion associated with public sermons. Some of these poems are close to conventional moralizing, while others relentlessly push the limits of imagery. The inclusion of this category is useful in reminding the reader of the ritual and communal contexts of Sufism.

71. Which Earth Lacks You?

Like poem 62, this poem explores the contradictions of the limited spatial imagination. If God is everywhere, what are the practical implications?

> Which earth lacks you? So that
>   they look up seeking you in heaven?
> You'll see them gazing at you in public,
>   though they blindly fail to see you.

72. Beware Consolation

In *News of Hallaj* narrative 55, Hallaj introduces this poem by saying, "Whoever wishes to reach the goal should leave the world behind his back." Despite an initial distrust of unexpected experiences, the poem ends with paradoxical reflections on the part and the whole.

> Beware consolation, my soul!
> > For power is from denial and surrender.
> Beware the dawning that appears from
> > the niche of unveiled manifestation.
> A part of me is based on part of my part,
> > but all of me longs for all of my all.

73. This World Deceives Me

In the spirit of ascetic poems that blame the world, these verses brim with contempt for mundane temptations.

> This world deceives me as though
>> I didn't know its condition.
> God outlawed its forbidden things,
>> while I avoid its lawful things.
> Its right hand stretches out to me,
>> but I reject it, even its left hand!
> I saw that it was in need,
>> so I gave it all of itself.
> 5 When would I have known union with it,
>> so that I would fear being bored with it?

74. The Steeds of Separation

An allegorical poem with courtly overtones, this is a sermon in verse on the theme of the militant soul defending its virtue.

> When the steeds of separation descend on you
>> and despair calls for the end of hope,
> Seize with your left the shield of humility
>> and grab with the right the sword of weeping.
> By your soul, your soul, beware,
>> and be alert to the betraying ambush.
> If loneliness comes at you in the dark,
>> then travel with the lamps of pure light.
> Say to your lover, "Do you see my lowliness?
>> Be generous, forgive me before our meeting!"
> In the name of love, don't turn away
>> from your beloved, except when desire is requited.

75. Pilgrim's Prayer

This poem begins with the pilgrim's salutation to God (*labbayka*) that is an established part of the hajj, providing ritual overtones to a love poem. Parts of this poem (verses 7, 10, 13, and 14) recall conventional hyperbolic tropes of suffering lovers, already well-established in the poetry of Abu Nuwas. The first six verses are a dialogue between lovers, making metaphysical claims about the all. This section is followed by two verses of ambivalence, and then three on the analogy of love and medicine. The lover then despairs of his failure, like a drowning man, but his complaint turns into resignation. The last three verses address the beloved hopelessly.

> I am here, my secret and my confidant,
> > I am here, my object and my meaning.
> I call you, or you call me to you—or is it
> > I who called to you, or you whispered to me?
> Eye of the eye of my being, aspiration's limit,
> > my language, my expressions, my gesture,
> All of my all, my hearing, and my vision,
> > everything of me, my limbs and parts,
> 5   All of my all, though all of the all is concealed,
> > and all of your all is covered by my meaning—
> You to whom my spirit clings! It has been destroyed
> > in ecstasy, so I've become the pawn of my desires.
> I cry in sorrow for my separation from home,
> > submissively; even my enemies help me lament!
> I approach, but my fear drives me away, and a longing
> > torments me, settling in my inner guts.
> What can I do with a lover I've fallen for,
> > my Lord? Even my doctors are sick of my illness.
> 10   They said, "Treat it with Him!" So I said to them,
> > "People! Can you treat the disease with the disease?"
> My love for my Lord consumes me and weakens me,
> > but how can I complain to my Lord of my Lord?
> I gaze at him, and my heart knows him,
> > but nothing expresses him except my gesture.
> Woe to my spirit, for my spirit, and alas for my grief,
> > for myself, from me, for I am indeed the source of my suffering,

As though I were one drowning, whose fingertips appear,
    In desperation, in the midst of the watery deep.
15   None knows what I have encountered from anyone,
    except the one who has dwelled in me, in the center of my heart.
He truly knows how much I've wasted away,
    and my life and death are by his wish.
Goal of my quest, my hope, and my rest,
    life of my spirit, my religion, and my world,
Tell me, for I am your ransom, oh my hearing, and my sight:
    Why do you insist on my exile and banishment?
Although you are hidden from my eyes behind a veil,
    still the heart attends to you from far away.

76. How Long Do You Contest

Here is a stern sermon, with a strong emphasis on reproaching the sinner.

> How long do you contest the one who sees you
> > in a sea of errors, though you don't see him?
> Your way should be piety and religion,
> > but your deed is the deed of the voluptuous.
> You think that you are free from any sin,
> > but God's eye is the witness that observes you.
> Do you desire forgiveness for your sins?
> > Yet you don't even seek his satisfaction.
> 5   Can you be happy with your sins and errors,
> > forgetting him, when there is no other?
> Repent before you die, before the day
> > when slaves encounter what their hands have done.

77. Intellect's Advice

In *News of Hallaj* narrative 62, in response to a question about the divine unity, Hallaj reflects on the inadequacy of any human proclamation. These verses then express his suspicion of the capacity of reason to prove God.

> One who seeks him asking intellect's advice—
> > God grants him an astonishment that he enjoys.
> He has mixed his secrets with deception,
> > saying in his astonishment, "Does he exist?"

78. Song of Death

This poem occurs in *News of Hallaj* narrative 2, following a lengthy prayer offered by Hallaj the night before he was killed. This lament features an unusual anaphora or repeated formula in the first six verses, with the poet crying in funereal despair from the devastating experience of witnessing eternity and revelation. The perception of the realm beyond "how" is limited to the "witness of eternity"—that is, Hallaj (as Shaybi described him). The poem then shifts to a lament for the failure of language, memory, speech, and allusion in the face of this reality; Shaybi considers it a lament for the decline of Sufism. The two concluding verses (missing in Sarraj's version) invoke Qur'anic images of cities that God destroyed for rejecting the prophets, and the depiction of the Meccan pagans as blindly following the herd in their ignorance. The overall effect is a somber reflection on the impossibility of comprehending God, combined with a complaint about the decline of the age. There is a certain irony in this cosmic death announcement given by Hallaj on the eve of his execution.

> I cry to you the death of souls whose witness went astray;
>   in what is beyond "how," one meets eternity's witness.
> I cry to you the death of hearts, as long as clouds
>   of revelation pour down seas of wisdom upon them.
> I cry to you the death of truth's language, for long ago
>   it died, and its imagined memory is like nothing.
> I cry to you the death of rhetoric, and the surrender
>   of every orator's words, in speech of understanding.
> 5   I cry to you the death of all thinkers' allusions;
>   nothing remains of them but the erasing of their bones.
> I cry the death, by your love! of the ethics of a people
>   whose steeds were just the sorrow of repression.
> All of them are gone; neither essence nor trace remains,
>   like the passing of 'Ad and the destruction of Iram.
> They follow the crowd, imitating their fashion,
>   dumber than cattle, and dumber than a beast of burden.

79. Guidance of the Lost

Here is another brief sermon, this one calling for repentance.

> You who ignore the way of guidance's paths—
> > for what rests on Truth has a place to stand—
> Give up the path of ignorance and turn toward
> > a Lord who holds the deeds that are renewed.

VI.
Riddles

The riddle is a literary form that was quite popular in Arabic, as it was in many other languages. The poems of this type that are credited to Hallaj pose a series of questions that must be answered with letters of the Arabic alphabet that together form the word that is the ultimate goal. The distinctive feature here is the theological and mystical character of the answers. But it would be a mistake to ignore the undercurrent of competition signaled by the author's challenge to the ingenious reader.

80. There Are Four Letters

A riddle to which the answer is "Allah" (comprised of the four Arabic letters A, L, L, H).

> There are four letters that my heart desires,
> > obliterating my ambitions and my thought.
> An A that inclines creatures
> > to his creation, and an L that runs to blame.
> Then one more L to emphasize those meanings,
> > then an H that I desire—can you guess?

81. Three Letters without Dots

In *News of Hallaj* narrative 39, this poem is the culmination of an ecstatic session; the answer to the riddle is *tawhid* ("affirming unity").

> Three letters without dots,
>> then two dotted, and the speech is done.
> One dotted letter resembles his ecstatic lovers,
>> and everyone affirms the one that's left.
> The other letters are a ciphered riddle,
>> for there is no travel here, nor any station.

82. You Who Are Unaware

A context for this poem is provided by *News of Hallaj* narrative 40, where some prominent Sufis of Baghdad challenge Hallaj to a debate; the poem is his defiant response, in which he claims an exalted spiritual rank. A hagiographic emphasis follows as Hallaj performs miracles of healing and telekinesis. Several solutions have been proposed for the riddle, the most likely being "my law [*namusi*] [is that] I am Moses [*ana Musa*]."

> You who are unaware in ignorance of my rank,
>   do you know nothing of my reality and my story?
> For my worship of God is six letters,
>   among which there are two with dots [*N, Y*].
> Two are consonants: one a root [*M*], another [*S*] with its vowel
>   in spelling related to "my faith" [*imani*].
> And if the chief of letters [*A*] appears before them,
>   a letter standing in the place of the second letter,
> 5   you'll view me standing in the place of Moses,
>   in the light above Sinai when you see me.

83. Return to God

A context for this poem is furnished by a story (*News of Hallaj*, no. 46) that depicts Hallaj miraculously detecting someone about to spend money unlawfully; Hallaj counsels him to give the money instead in alms. When asked, "Where did you find this out?" Hallaj replies as follows: "Every heart that is emptied of whatever is other than God sees His concealment in the hidden and His contents in the secret." When pressed for further advice, Hallaj answers, "Whoever seeks God from the *mim* and the `*ayn* [of *ma`a*, "with"] finds Him, and whoever seeks Him between the *alif* and the *nun* in the letter of connection [i.e., *ya*'; the three letters together spell *ayna*, "where"] loses Him. For He is sanctified from the difficulties of conjectures and He is exalted above the thoughts of the clever." The poem then follows as an explication of this short sermon. The narrative thus presents Hallaj as possessing supernatural knowledge because of his detachment from all that is other than God. His counsel is that God must be sought in intimate conjunction ("with") rather than in space ("where"), which implies separation. The language used to describe God ("sanctified," "exalted") is typical of the theological creeds that define God's transcendence, yet the notion of human union with God is ironically present throughout this passage, which concludes, paradoxically, with the revelation of spatial dimensions.

> Return to God, for God is the goal,
>> and when you've reached the end, there is no God but he.
> For he is *with* the creatures to whom he belongs,
>> in the letters of "*with*," which mean "to sanctify."
> Its meaning is on the lips of one who unravels a knot
>> from its spelling for people who only pronounce it.
> If you doubt, think of the saying of your Master,
>> so that he says, against your doubt, "This is he!"
> 5 By the first letter, he is shown in height and depth;
>> by the last letter, he is shown both far and near.

84. Suggestion and Expression

Shaybi rightly comments that this poem is "extremely intractable." It has the appearance of a letter riddle, but there is no solution. It begins as an epistolary exercise ("I wrote," as in no. 101) but the terms of reference are quickly deconstructed into isolated letters. The poem concludes with the formula of monotheistic deification—"he is He" (*huwa huwa*)—as an articulation of transcendence.

> I wrote to him with an understood suggestion
>   and intimately explored the language of expression,
> In a letter for him, from him, by him, to him,
>   translating a hidden lore of veiling,
> With the *U* of union and the *P* of proof,
>   the *M* of modesty and the *P* of purity,
> The *L* of loyalty, the *C* of cleanliness,
>   and an *L* and *F* revolving round a life,
> 5   In a hidden secret as heart's ecstasy,
>   and the *H* of hidden, the *S* of suggestion—
> Creatures belong to God as an ultimate truth,
>   by a right when the truth of the visit is proved,
> By them, not by them, since they are not they,
>   though there is no lofty feature but them.
> For all are by all, the whole of the whole,
>   from the all by the all, the word of a day.
> It is clay, and fire, and light, because
>   the answer responds to the expression.
> 10   And He remains who was there, before there was place,
>   comprehending everything in knowledge as His abode.
> For He instantly raises up his enemies
>   among jinn and men in heat as a fire,
> And He settles his friends in his vicinity,
>   with wonderful grace and beautiful freshness.
> For he is He, the original origin of origins,
>   and he is He, the time of times of eternity.

VII.
The Spiritual Path

This substantial group of poems focuses on issues relating to spiritual practice and contemplation as they were emerging in the nascent Sufi movement. In several places (poems 85, 90, and 92), Hallaj dwells on the nature of esoteric terminology and on the consequences of breaking the discipline of secrecy, consequences that included the condemnation of many Sufi leaders. These poems also explore approaches toward God, who is either conceived spatially, as ascension, or described psychologically, through images of ecstasy and drunkenness. These experiences are presented as a discovery of the self's inner realities, which are increasingly elusive the closer one comes.

85. Silence

This poem is a reflection on the Sufis' technical language, which offers precision to insiders but also excludes the uninitiated. Terms are arranged in rough clusters of three. Not really a *qasida*, the poem ends in affirmation of community.

> Silence, then taciturnity, then dumbness;
>> and knowledge, then finding, then burying;
> And clay, then fire, then light;
>> and cold, then shadow, then sun;
> And hard ground, then coast, then desert;
>> and river, then ocean, then dry;
> And drunk, then sober, then longing;
>> and proximity, then union, then intimacy;
> And contraction, then expansion, then vanishing;
>> and separation, then joining, then extinction.
> These are expressions for the people to whom
>> the world is equivalent to a penny.
> And they are voices beyond the door, but
>> even nearby the words of mortals mumble.
> The last of things to which a man returns,
>> when he reaches the limit, are destiny and self.
> For mortals are the slaves of their desires,
>> and the truth of Truth is holy when made sacred.

86. You're the Viewpoint

This extraordinary poem features the strongest qualities of Hallaj's poetic style. The perspective deliberately and subtly shifts in the opening, addressed to a "you," which is both the author's other self and an undiscovered country. "Tangled words" play on the relationships of the all, the part, and the rest to one another. The third verse abruptly swivels to the reader, who is invited to mourn for the now remote and impersonal image of the author, powerfully portrayed as being ravished, his heart carried off in the claws of a bird of prey. The last half of the poem follows the elusive remains of a self that is scattered before infinite divine power, depicted as astonishment in the desert. Yet the self still remains sufficiently present to witness its own near disappearance.

> You're the viewpoint from which I gaze,
>> but you're the place that's secret from my mind.
> You're the all of the all, the all of which
>> is dearer to me than part of me or the rest of me—
> Can you see yourself mourning for him
>> whose heart is grasped by the claws of a bird?
> Madly in love, bewildered, rendered savage,
>> he flees from one desert to another.
> He steals forth unconsciously, while his secrets
>> steal forward like a blazing flash of lightning,
> As imagination's speed to one imagining
>> the subtleness of ancient mystery,
> In the abyss of the ocean of thought, where
>> flow graces from the power of the Almighty.

87. The Condition of Knowledge

This didactic piece of advice rests on the observation that beginners in contemplation are easily distracted by undisciplined gazes. To attain true knowledge requires erasing everything from the heart except God.

> The condition of knowledge is to erase everything from you; for
> the disciple starts with a glance that's unaware.

88. Dualities

This poem uses contrasting pairs to signal a series of dilemmas in the first three verses. But in the remainder of the poem, these dualities are viewed from the perspective of one who has transcended them. The hinge of the poem is verse 4, where the reader is invited to attend to the symbolic presentation that follows, depicting the riddle of human existence in tension with its eternal origin. After a lengthy series of paradoxes, the poem concludes with two verses that evoke a spiritual community formed by the primordial covenant between human souls and God.

> Knowledge has its owners, and faith has an order,
> yet knowledge and its owners have experiences.
> Knowledge is of two kinds: rejected and acquired.
> And the sea is of two kinds: well-traveled and avoided.
> Time is of two kinds: one condemned, one praised.
> People are of two kinds: privileged and dispossessed.
> Now listen with your heart to what a friend conveys to you,
> and consider with your reason, for discernment is a gift.
>
> 5   I climbed the mountaintop without taking a step;
> its heights pose risks for anyone else.
> I dove into an ocean without wetting my feet;
> my spirit plunged in, though my heart was afraid.
> Its grains of sand are jewels that no hand has approached,
> though understanding's grasp can plunder them.
> I drank my fill of water without a mouth,
> though it is water that has been drunk by mouths,
> Because my spirit has thirsted for it eternally,
> while the body didn't touch it before its own creation.
>
> 10 I am an orphan, and I have a father I take refuge in,
> and my heart suffers as long as I live, absent from him.
> Blind yet visionary, I'm a fool, but clever,
> and my speech turns backward when I wish.
> Certain youths know now what I have learned, for they
> are my friends, since the good have friendship.
> They recognized themselves in the eternal beginning;
> their sun is dawning, while time is darkening.

89. The Wings of My Intention

These verses present a concise symbolic depiction of an ascension to the highest heaven. The poem concludes by evoking the annihilation of self. Yet is that limit ever reached? The deserts of nearness are distinctly inhospitable.

> My glance gestured with the eye of knowledge
> > toward a pure essence, with my hidden thought.
> And a light flashed in my awareness, subtler
> > than the understanding of my fanciful ambition.
> So I dove into the wave of my thought's ocean,
> > passing through it just like an arrow.
> And my heart flew with a feathered longing
> > mounted on the wings of my intention,
> 5 Toward him for whom, if I'm asked about him,
> > I provide a symbol, but I don't name him.
> Until, when I crossed over every limit
> > I wept in the deserts of nearness.
> I looked, and there I was, in a book [of destiny],
> > but I could not get beyond the limit of my record.
> So I went on, in submission to him,
> > with the rope of my guidance in the hand of resignation.
> Love has imprinted my heart with him,
> > with the brand of longing—and what an imprint!
> 10 Awareness of my essence faded away
> > in nearness, until I forgot my name.

90. Keeping the Secret

This remarkable composition addresses head-on the question of esoteric secrecy and the penalty for exposing it to the public. With a clear admission of his own responsibility for this crime, Hallaj somberly warns others of the results of his path. If one takes the poem literally, as many transmitters do, this becomes a confession of the sin of breaking discipline, as Hallaj admits in verse 6. Yet the poem can also be read ironically, as a warning to avoid his fate. This relatively short composition displays symmetry, with nearly the same formula in verses 1 and 6 ("One they confide in. . . . One whom they tell a secret") allowing Hallaj to publically admit that he is the one accused of revealing the secret. The key term for this sin, "reveal," occurs at both beginning and end (verse 2, mirrored by verses 8 and 9). The last section (verses 7–9) describes the community of Sufis by exclusions, with four clauses introduced by a negation ("no," "won't," "don't"), before the final verse turns to the reader with advice.

> One they confide in, who blurts out all that they concealed
>   and maintains no connection, is nothing but a swindler.
> If souls reveal the secret of what they have learned
>   and everything their intellect acquired—beware!
> One who fails to protect the secret of his Lord and Master
>   they will not trust with secrets while he lives.
> They punish him for misdeeds of the past
>   and make him trade society for loneliness.
> 5   They avoid him, for he's not fit for their company,
>   since they see him as a grave robber of secrets.
> One whom they tell a secret, which he then betrays,
>   that one, like me, is frivolous to these people.
> They are people of a secret, created for secrets,
>   and they have no patience for what is obscene.
> They won't welcome a revealer in their assemblies,
>   and they don't love a veil that's treated lightly.
> They will not choose a revealer of their secrets.
>   Beware of their majesty—of that beware!
> 10   So be with them and for them in every misfortune,
>   polite to them as long as you last.

91. The Claim of Poverty

This is a critique of the narrow asceticism that sees poverty as a proof of spiritual status.

> You claim that you would reach him by poverty and need,
> > but poverty is your pleasure, so take away its goals!
> Poverty is the lowest station of those who are ascetic for his sake,
> > like the child who is weaned from what it enjoys.

92. The Secrets of Truth

Here is another didactic verse, warning novices that there are many divine
secrets they are not ready for.

> The secrets of Truth do not appear to the veiled.
> He hides it from you, so don't oppose the one who hides it.
> Don't worry about what you do not comprehend;
> God forbid that reality should appear, and then you claim him!

93. He Opened the Veil

This poem is a dense meditation on the shortcomings of ecstasy as an approach to God. It begins with the annihilation of all signs and meanings in the divine presence, a formula repeated in the opening and closing verses. The poem concludes with the limitations of burning ecstasy and its transitory character.

> He opened the veil, and humbled with His majesty
>   the power of signs, and all imagined meaning.
> How wrong that He be grasped in ecstasy!
>   Burning ecstasy is the feeble sign of weakness.
> Ecstasy grasps nothing but a vanished sign,
>   and ecstasy vanishes when the vision comes.
> I delighted in ecstasy, though fearfully—
>   sometimes it hides me, other times I'm present.
> He wipes out ecstasy for those who witness Him;
>   he wipes out ecstasy, and all remembered meaning.

94. Drunk and Sober

Here Hallaj plays with the binary opposition between intoxication and sobriety, two qualities that Sufi hagiographies often assign separately to Hallaj and his onetime master Junayd. That apparent duality seems to be overstated, however.

> Is it enough for you that sobriety revealed you?
>> But what of the drunken state, when drunkenness is better?
> Your two states are my two states: drunk and sober.
>> I'll stay in my two states, both drunk and sober.

95. Jealousy of God

This poem displays the tension between affirmative and negative theologies—the former revealing God by signs and allusions, the latter indicating what God is not. While both are necessary, it is the positive remembrance that is the source of ecstasy.

> If I wished, I'd show my secrets by my secrets
> > and reveal ecstasy in my conscience and my self.
> But I'm jealous of one who knows my Lord,
> > only knowing him by way of negation.
> My allusions come from God, despite the growing gap
> > between creation's income and expense.
> Your light never shined for me for a day so I could confirm it
> > without me negating it by some denial.
> 5   I've never remembered you without raving from delight,
> > so that I tear my guts and rags apart.

96. Total Fusion

Prayer presupposes distance, seeking to overcome it with union. This poem rests in the unstable space between.

"My Lord!" is the cry of one who's seeking
    your nearness in your distance, and your comfort.
You've already revealed the forms of meaning,
    showing them in clothes of manifestation.
You've turned my limbs from every other purpose,
    so all of me is totally with you.

97. Vision of the End

This poem is quoted by Ruzbihan in the midst of an extensive meditation on the execution of Hallaj. It has the character of a presentiment of martyrdom, which is both a funeral and a wedding. Ruzbihan comments that this is a description of a vision of the angelic realm, which he regards as a well-established phenomenon.

> When the whisper came
>   of the funeral and the wedding,
> I saw the garden and the fire,
>   the angels and the throne.

VIII.
Union

Using a term like "union" might imply a dogmatic theology that asserts the unity of God and humanity. Such a stiff formulation hardly does justice to the delicate explorations of the foundations of the self that these poems reveal. Nevertheless, it seems legitimate to use union as an asymptotic limit, a line that is glimpsed and approached but never crossed. The emotional intensity of these poems betrays a fundamental instability in the relationship of love, and the annihilation of the ego is glimpsed hopefully without being finally attained. Here Hallaj plays with concepts like the "indwelling" (*hulul*) of the spirit, which was over-read—and condemned—as a theological declaration of the Christian doctrine of incarnation. But it would be a mistake to see these poems as theological doctrine; Hallaj insists upon the limits of reasoned explanation, even as he uses the emotional powers of language to express unresolvable dilemmas.

98. Is It You or I?

This piece is the culmination of *News of Hallaj* narrative 50, an account that places Hallaj in a Baghdad mosque, begging the people to put him to death, much to their consternation. The narrator of this episode follows Hallaj home and asks him about the path to God. Hallaj replies, "The path is between two, but there is no other with God," and then launches into this poem as a defiance of duality. Later commentators see here the basis for understanding the Hallajian declaration "I am the Truth" as the description of the annihilation of the ego, the removal of "I am" from in between.

> Is it you or I? That would be two gods in me;
> > far, far be it from you to assert duality!
> The "he-ness" that is yours is in my nothingness forever;
> > my "all" added to your "all" would be a double disguise.
> But where is your essence, from my vantage point when I see you,
> > since my essence has become plain in the place where I am not?
> And where is your face? It is the object of my gaze,
> > whether in my inmost heart or in the glance of my eye.
> 5   Between you and me there is an "I am" that battles me,
> > so take away, by your grace, this "I am" from in between.

99. His Memory Is Mine

This verse is quoted in *Tawasin* 6:15, in a passage presenting the dialogue of Moses and Iblis on Mount Sinai. There Iblis explains that his pure mono-theism caused him to disobey God's command to prostrate before Adam, which would have been idolatry. Moses then asks Iblis whether he remembers the God who threw him out of paradise. Iblis replies, "Moses, memory is not remembered; I am the remembered, and he is the remembered." He then recites this verse. This is a key text for the counterintuitive view of Iblis as the selfless lover of God.

> His memory is mine, and my memory is his;
>   can there be two who remember, except as one?

100. Mixing Spirits

Here is an explicitly physical metaphor for union, expressed as the mixture of perfumes.

> Your spirit has mixed with my spirit, as
>   ambergris is mixed with aromatic musk.
> If anything touches you, it touches me,
>   and since you are me, we do not differ.

101. I Wrote You

This piece, which occurs in *News of Hallaj* (no. *3), is traditionally depicted as the end of a letter from Hallaj to a fellow Sufi, Ibn `Ata', who was himself beaten to death by the authorities for his support of Hallaj. This kind of letter forms part of the culture of intimacy within Sufi circles, in which writing letters filled with poetry played a major role.

> I wrote you, but I didn't write you;
>> I only wrote my spirit, without a letter.
> That's because the spirit is not separated
>> from its lovers by a closing word.
> So every letter coming from and reaching you
>> without reply is my reply.

102. My Unique One

This poem appears to contain the phrase indelibly associated with Hallaj, "I am the Truth" (*ana al-haqq*), although some scholars have offered different readings and changed their minds about the text. It is in fact difficult to establish just when and how Hallaj may have used the phrase, which was not even discussed in his heresy trial. The poem begins with a declaration about being chosen in relation to the transcendent one, a paradoxical connection. The cool and ironic claim to union that follows is tempered by the ambiguity of Hallaj's continuing presence as a cover or clothing despite the lack of separation. The concluding line celebrates with blazing illumination.

> My unique one chose me for a unique truth,
>> one to which no path leads.
> For I am the Truth, a truth that Truth deserved,
>> clothing its essence with no more separation.
> Rising suns have manifested, shining,
>> glittering, and the rising suns are lightning!

103. Your Place in My Heart

Here is another declaration of total dedication including both body and soul.

> Your place in my heart is all of my heart,
>   and no one else is able to take your place.
> My spirit places you between my skin and bones—
>   so how do you think I'll do if I lose you?

104. Your Spirit Was Mixed

These verses provide a variation on the metaphor of mixture, this time with liquids instead of fragrances (as in poem 100).

> Your spirit was mixed in my spirit,
>   just like wine and clear water.
> If something touches you, it touches me,
>   for you are I in every state.

105. I Have Pretended Patience

This poem offers a declaration of union with the beloved, despite dissonance within the soul.

> I have pretended patience; but can my heart
>> be patient with my soul?
> Your spirit has mixed with my spirit
>> in my nearness and my distance,
> So I am you, just as you
>> are me, and my desire.

106. Glory to the One

The intimacy of these verses aroused the condemnation of critics such as Ibn Taymiyya, who saw here a heretical incarnationism equivalent to Christianity. Nevertheless, Sufi interpreters viewed this poem as a profound evocation of the divine unity and its manifestation in the world.

> Glory to the one whose humanity displayed
> > the brilliant secret of his bright godhood!
> Then he appeared openly to his creation
> > in the form of one who eats and drinks,
> So that his people looked on him
> > like the wink of one eyelid to another.

107. I Am the One That I Desire

Possibly the most famous verse attributed to Hallaj, this poem masterfully describes the goal of union in the most basic terms.

> I am the one that I desire, the one I desire is I;
>> we are two spirits dwelling in a single body.
> So when you have seen me, you have seen him,
>> and when you have seen him, you have seen us.

108. You Are Flowing

Here is another meditation on union, concluding with praise of symmetry.

You are flowing between breast and heart,
    like the tears flowing from my eyes.
And you dwell in my consciousness, within my heart,
    like the spirits that dwell in bodies.
When one at rest begins to move, it's only
    you who move him, from a hidden place.
You're the moon, shining at fourteen days,
    made of eight plus four plus two.

109. I Entered into Creation

In *News of Hallaj* narrative 53, this poem serves as the conclusion of an emotional theological description of God's transcendence and the ambiguities of revelation. Here (as in poem 106) Hallaj plays with the Christian-sounding vocabulary of humanity and divinity, flirting with incarnational themes. Yet the divine manifestation is given to some but not others. The poem concludes with the apocalyptic imagery of reversing the order of nature (the sun rising in the west and setting in the east), but only as a metaphor for the catastrophe of being deprived of the divine presence.

> I entered into creation with my humanity, for you;
>> if it weren't for you, my divinity, I would have fled sincerity.
> For the language of knowledge is for speech and guidance,
>> but the language of the hidden goes beyond speech.
> You showed yourself to a people, but hid from certain youths,
>> for they stray and wander, so you vanished from creation.
> So sometimes you rise for hearts in the west,
>> and then again for eyes you set in the east.

110. He Chose Me

Here is another declaration of total fusion with the divine.

He chose me, drew me near, and honored me.
The all advised me and taught me by the all.
No part remains between my heart and guts without
me knowing him by it, and him knowing me.

111. I Don't Play with Unity

Serious yet insouciant, this poem contrasts the experience of unity with God with its mere assertion, viewing rational proof as totally inadequate (as in poem 77).

> I don't play with divine unity
> > except when I ignore it.
> How can I ignore, how can I play,
> > if it is true that I am he?

112. Hiding

These verses present the fundamental dilemma of prayer, the choice between presence and separation.

> Your image is in my eye, your recollection is in my mouth,
> your abode is in my heart—so where are you hiding?

113. Secret of My Secret

When confronted with the experience of a God that is both beyond imagination and manifest everywhere, one has no excuse. Union is inescapable.

> Secret of my secret, you are so subtle,
>   you hide from all living imaginations.
> And you appear both without and within,
>   in everything, and through everything.
> And my excuse to you is only ignorance,
>   great doubt, and utter weakness.
> Totality of the all, you are not my other,
>   so in that case, what is my excuse to me?

114. Theory of Existence

This poem, which Massignon classifies as a *qasida*, has a distinctive formal structure exhibiting repetition, parallelism, and symmetrical construction. Three verses (1, 3, and 4) begin with negations, four begin with a demonstrative "this" (2, 7, 8, and 9), while the central verses (5 and 6) use the piling up of prepositions that characterizes Hallaj's negative theology. The repetition of the formula "for him, from him, to him, by him" at the center of the poem announces that these Hallajian technical terms are the key to its meaning. And the term "explanation" is repeated both at the end of the first half line and at the end of verse 6, signaling that there is an explanation—expressed in this poem, one assumes. While the poem begins with a single voice, the final lines affirm the community of "his ecstatic seekers," defined in effect by their shared language. This poem's upbeat presentation of the Sufis forms a stark contrast to the somber lament of poem 90, where Hallaj reflects on their rejection of him for having publicized the secret.

> My explanation does not stand between me and the Truth,
> > nor is there proof by signs or evidence.
> This is the manifestation of Truth's dawn: a burning
> > that shines with power in its radiance.
> None knows the Truth but one who is made to know;
> > vanishing time cannot know the eternal.
> One doesn't prove the Creator by his work;
> > have you seen a creature reveal the times?
> 5 The proof was for him, from him, to him, by him,
> > from Truth's witness in a scripture's descent.
> The proof was for him, from him, by him, for him,
> > truth that we discovered, knowledge explained.
> This is my finding, my comment, my belief;
> > it's what unifies my unity and faith.
> These words are the expression of ascetics,
> > who know things secretly and openly.
> This is the true finding of his ecstatic seekers,
> > the like-minded—my friends and companions.

115. Concentration and Separation

This poem reflects on the tension between the state of concentration on God in pre-creational eternity, and the separation and distraction of life in the world of time; this dialectic is also expressed as losing and finding oneself. It suggests the importance of meditation on the primordial encounter with God, experienced as a departure from ordinary consciousness. The concluding lines illustrate the paradoxical results of that concentration on pre-eternity, transforming the absence of separation into presence.

> Concentration lost them to themselves in eternity;
> > separation found them for a time, without a trace.
> Their souls departed, and for them departing
> > concentrated evidence far from people.
> Their concentration wipes out formal qualities,
> > from the effects of rapture in the other.
> Time's condition vanishes in their eternity,
> > hidden without forms from concentration's evidence,
> 5   But they received in separation everything
> > that drew them when they were in his presence.
> Thus concentration is their absence; separation is their presence.
> > Loss and finding are visible either way.

116. How Will Union Take Place?

The established convention of the lover's complaint takes on new dimensions when the dialectic between union and rejection involves annihilation of the self.

> Unite me in union, my love,
>> but unite in a union without accusation.
> You claim that I am annihilated from myself—
>> so how can I become close to myself?
> If the heart that is mine approaches you,
>> don't question me, but just ask it about me,
> A question that is attentive and protective:
>> the truth is what I mean—and do you mean it?
> 5 My love, by that rejection, even if
>> by reason of rejection, unite me!
> And don't kill me with the worry of rejection,
>> for the blow of rejections is exhausting.
> I'm amazed that I'm dying of longing
>> while you, my Lord, abandon me.

117. Perfect Satisfaction

Here is a final reflection on love as astonishment, surrender, and sacrifice.
The poem concludes by invoking the community of lovers.

> My beloved, you're my wish,
>   and you may see me in my place.
> Your light truly is dazzling
>   to my vision, for my vision,
> And I've proved your truth, so do
>   everything you wish to me.
> For I am killed in love and
>   am annihilated with the lovers.

NOTES ON THE POEMS

1. The Ardent Renouncer

kafā ḥazanan . . . ghā'ibu (Shaybi² 202, Massignon¹ M8, W 110)

Transmitted in the Sufi Qur'an commentaries of Ibn ʿAta' and Sulami (on Qur'an 3:188), and also by Khargushi and the fourteenth-century Egyptian alchemist ʿIzz al-Din al-Jildaki.

Verse 2. "favor" (*al-faḍl*): "union" (*al-waṣl*), another MS.

"and I've seen none like me renouncing, while desiring" (*fa-lam ara mithlī zāhidan wa-huwa rāghibu*): "none before me has been seen to renounce you while desiring" (*fa-lam yura qablī zāhidun fīka rāghibu*), various MSS.

2. Gathering Desire after Separation

kānat li-qalbī ahwā' . . . ahwāya (Shaybi² 403, Massignon¹ M3, W 105)

Quoted by Qushayri, Ruzbihan, Ibn al-Dabbagh, Ghazali, al-ʿAmuli, Subki, and others. Shaybi considers this an attributed poem, noting its similarity to verses found in the conventional love poetry of the Baghdadian poet Abu Nuwas and of Ibn Daud, author of the anthology *The Book of the Flower* (*Kitab al-zahra*). Nevertheless, its wide circulation indicates its popularity among Sufis.

3. Strengthen Me from the Sickness

naẓarī bad'u ʿillatī . . . janā (Shaybi² 165, Massignon¹ C12, W 224)

Transmitted in Muhammad ibn Abu al-Fadl al-Hamadani's *Takmila ta'rikh al-Tabari*, a supplement (composed in 1094) to Tabari's universal history *Ta'rikh al-rusul wal-muluk* (written in 914). Massignon considers this a later poem in the style of Hallaj, but Shaybi and others accept it.

Verse 1. "what it committed" (*mā janā*): "though it did not sin" (Qasim Mir Akhuri), taking *mā* as a negation.

Verse 2. "sickness" (*ḍanā*): "annihilation" (*fanā'*), twice.

4. Dialogue of the Heart with the Truth

ra'aytu rabbī . . . anta (Shaybi² 216, Massignon¹ M10, W 112; *Tawasin* 5:11–12, ed. Nwyia, 200)

These verses can be found quoted by Hujwiri, Suhrawardi, Ibn al-ʿArif, al-Qaysari, al-Nabulsi, Ibn ʿArabi, anonymously in al-Damiri's *Life of Animals*, and in *Madkhal tashwiq al-ghafilin*, a Judeo-Arabic work by Sa`id ibn Da'ud al-`Adani; the latter's reading is preferred by Shaybi. Some, like the prominent North African Sufi Ibn `Ajiba (d. 1809), attribute the poem to the Prophet's cousin `Ali. But there is also an anonymous hagiography of Abu Yazid al-Bistami, cited by `Abd al-Rahman al-Badawi, *Shatahat al-sufiyya*, that credits him instead.

Verse 1. "and he said, 'Who are you?' I said, 'You.'" (*fa-qāla man anta fa-qultu anta*), Nwyia: "so I said, there is no doubt—it's you! You!" (*fa-qultu lā shakka anta anta*), al-`Adani, Shaybi.

Verse 4. "imagination" (*wahm*): "time" (*dahr*), *Tawasin* 5:12, ed. Massignon, p. 31.

5. First the Guest, Then the House

sakanta qalbī . . . al-jāru (Shaybi[2] 453, Massignon[1] M23, W 126)

Shaybi[2] points out that this poem is found in the *Diwan* of the Mamluk poet al-Baha' Zuhayr (d. 1258).

6. Alchemical Expressions

yā nasīm al-rīḥi . . . illā `aṭashā (Shaybi[2] 290, Massignon[1] M32, W 135)

Quoted by Tawhidi, Raghib al-Isfahani, Ibn `Arabi's *Futuhat*, and Rumi's *Diwan* 264 and *Mathnawi* book 3 (alongside Hallaj no. 44, "Kill Me, Friends"). Massignon interprets the mixing of spirits as alchemical. This poem is performed by Syrian singer Abed Azrie.

Verse 1. "breeze" (*yā nasīm*): Shaybi[2] reads "breezes" (*nasamāt*), since a plural noun would fit the feminine gender of the verb. The vocative singular is attested, however, and is rhetorically preferable for a poem that intentionally evokes the conventional conceit of the messenger.

7. The Sun of Hearts

ṭala`at shamsun . . . ghurūbi (Shaybi[2] 197, Massignon[1] M9, W 111)

Quoted in the Qur'an commentaries of Sulami and Qushayri (on Qur'an 6:76), and also in Kharghushi, Hamadani's continuation of Tabari, Ibn Badis, Ibn `Ajiba, Ghazali, and `Izz al-Din Maqdisi.

Verse 1. "by night" (*bi-laylin*): "one night" (*laylatan*), another MS.

"glowed" (*istanārat*): "gleamed" (*istaḍā'at*), another MS.

Verse 2. "sets" (*taghrabu*), Wazin: "rises" (*taṭla`u*), Massignon.

Verse 3. Only found in Abu Hamid al-Ghazali, *Rawḍat al-ṭālibīn* (Cairo: Maktaba al-Jandi, n.d.), 132.

8. Religion of Lovers, and Religion of the People

wallāhi mā ṭala`at . . . bi-anfāsī (Shaybi[2] 459, Massignon[1] M31, W 134)

There is no indication in the earliest sources that this was ever considered to be a poem by Hallaj; Massignon must have included it mainly because he liked it. Hujwiri (*Kashf al-mahjub*, ed. Zhukovsky [Tehran: Tahuri, 1979], 565; trans. Nicholson, *Revealing the Mystery* [New York: Pir Press, 1999], 410), who knew Hallaj's poetry well, relates the first five verses of this poem anonymously, as something he heard from a wandering dervish in Azerbaijan who recited them and promptly died. The fact that Hujwiri does not consider this poem to be by Hallaj is telling. Al-Haskafi, a seventeenth-century Damascene jurist, relates all seven verses in a discussion about listening to music, again anonymously (*Ikhtiṣār al-fatāwā al-ṣūfiyya*, fol. 93a). The first to attribute this poem to Hallaj appears to have been the Timurid anthologist Mahmud Gazurgahi in his romanticized collection of Sufi biographies dedicated to Sultan Husayn Bayqara in 1503, *Majālis al-ʿushshāq* (p. 70), where it is claimed (contrary to all other narratives) that these verses were Hallaj's last words before his execution. The nineteenth-century Persian litterateur Rida Quli Khan Hidayat also credulously accepts this poem as being by Hallaj in his anthology *Riyāḍ al-ʿārifīn* (p. 119, four verses).

Massignon considers verse 5 to be derived from a line quoted by the ʿAbbasid literary anthologist Ibn Dawud, while lines 6 and 7 are versions of lines by Abu Nuwas; line 5 is also attributed to Abu Nuwas (Andras Hamori, "Love Poetry [Ghazal]," in *ʿAbbasid Belles-Lettres*, 213). Shaybi convincingly argues, on the basis of five similar poems in the same rhyme from ʿAbbasid anthologies, that this very conventional poem is falsely attributed to Hallaj.

Verse 2. "Sat apart" (*khalawtu*): "sat" (*jalastu*), Rida Quli.

Verse 4. The image reflected in the cup is a near duplicate of verse 6 in poem 2.

Verse 5. "gone to you" (*jiʾtukum*): "driven you away" (*nahartukum*), Haskafi.

"or" (*yā*): "not" (*lā*), Haskafi.

Verse 6. "painful" (*āsifan*): The textual reading (*wāsifan*, "peeling," a rare word) appears mistaken, and Wazin thinks it should be replaced with "sad" (*asifan*) or "painful" (*āsifan*).

Verse 7. "My religion's mine . . ." is an allusion to Qur'an 109:6, "You have your religion and I have my religion," a transparent claim that this love is a religion.

This poem has become popular on the internet as an anonymous devotional piece directed toward the Prophet Muhammad. It also became famous as one of the most popular songs featured in the 2012 Egyptian television serial *Al-Khawaga ʿAbd al-Qader*.

9. The Lover's Punishment

anā alladhī . . . ʿaliqat (Shaybi[2] 319, W 278)

Verse 5. "weaning" (*faṭm*): Hashim ʿUthman glosses this as an ending (*qaṭ*ʿ), while Shaybi simply registers surprise at this maternal term with a question mark. Nuin/Janés go overboard with nursing imagery, translating the line as "Even if my breast were exposed before a baby . . ."

10. The Cure of Love

anā saqīmun . . . bi-dawāk (Shaybi[2] 320, W 279)

Verse 4. Shaybi glosses *yuẓāhiru* as "departs" (*yughādiru, yuẓāyilu*).

11. Snakebite

al-sammu min . . . al-widāʿi (Meier 64/140)

In this poem, which Meier edited from the Zahabi codex in Shiraz (see appendix 4), the first two lines, with a slight variation, also occur in the *Diwan* of the Ottoman-era poet Ibn Zakur (d. 1708) (http://www.aldiwan.net/poem19795.html, accessed January 19, 2017). The same verses are attributed to Abu Turab ibn Jandal by al-Maqqari (d. 1632), the historian of Andalus, in *Nafh al-tib* (p. 222, http://islamport.com/w/adb/Web/2871 /1333.htm, accessed January 19, 2017). That in turn is quoted directly from another Andalusian author, Ibn Abbar (d. 1253) (*al-Takmila li-kitab al-sila*, 167, http://sh.bib -alex.net/tarikh/Web/6608/001.htm, accessed January 19, 2017).

Verse 2. "separation" (*firāq*): "farewell" (*widā`*), Ibn Jandal.

12. The Rule of Lovers

qaḍā `alayhi . . . yanami (Shaybi² 340, W 281)

Verse 1. Wazin remarks that the *ṣāb* is a tree whose sap is bitter.

13. Letter from the Depth of Spirit

inna kitābī . . . wa-ḍanā (Shaybi³ 90; W 284)

Verse 6. This line is fragmentary.

14. Where Is Your Match?

ṭūbā li-ṭarfin . . . naẓratayn (Shaybi³ 93, W 288)

15. The Veil of Invocation

anta al-muwallihu lī . . . dhikrī (Shaybi² 252, Massignon¹ M18, W 121)

This poem is quoted anonymously (as usual) by Kalabadhi in a discussion of the central Sufi concept of remembrance or recollection (*dhikr*); he comments, "This means that remembrance is the attribute of the rememberer, so if I disappear in my remembrance, my disappearance is in myself, and the only thing that veils the worshipper from his Lord is his own attributes" (*Ta`arruf* 1536). But Hallaj here does not so much recommend the ritual remembrance of God as he draws attention to the way it becomes an obstacle to direct contact with God.

On *walah* or "ravishing" as the highest level of love, see "The Stages of Love in Persian Sufism, from Rabi`a to Ruzbihan," in *The Heritage of Sufism*, Classical Persian Sufism from Its Origins to Rumi (700–1300), edited by Leonard Lewisohn, volume 1 (Oxford: One World, 1999), 435–55, especially 442.

Verse 2. "a means" (*wāsiṭa*): Some translators (Massignon in *Passion* 3:117, Dr. Javad Nurbakhsh, Akhuri) see here the metaphor of a central pearl (*wāsiṭa*) on a necklace, an image that connects to the "adornment" with which thought obscures remembrance. While the Muslim use of prayer beads (the *tasbīḥ*) probably dates from a period after the time of Hallaj, that does not detract from the image of a necklace of attributes that distracts the lover from a direct vision of the beloved.

16. Give Back to Me My Heart

antum malaktum . . . wādi (Shaybi² 233, Massignon¹ M16, W 119)

The plural address of this poem, in all three verses, registers as a departure from the singular beloved of standard love poetry; this formal tone also occurs in poem 28, "Burden of the Heart." The description of the poet as a "stranger" recalls the epithet of Hallaj as "the strange scholar" (*al-'ālim al-gharīb*, *Tawasin* 5:20), for which Massignon (*Passion*, 1:100) provides the Latin equivalents *Doctor Singularis* or *Doctor Exsul* (scholar of exile).

Verse 1. "I've wandered in every valley" (*fa-himtu fī kulli wādin*): an allusion to Qur'an 26:224–25, "the poets—the deluded follow them; have you not seen them wandering in every valley?" (*fī kulli wādin yahīmūna*).

Verse 2. "give back" (*raddū*): "is throbbing" (*wa-daqqa*), Massignon.

Verse 3. Though it is tempting to follow Stéphane Ruspoli's reading (*Le Message de Hallâj l'Expatrié: Recueil du Diwân, Hymnes et Prières, Sentences prophétiques et philosophiques* [Paris: Cerf, 2005], 201), "how long" (*bi-kam*) in place of "in you" (*bi-kum*), that would turn the final line into a clichéd question.

17. Constant Presence

ghibta wa-mā ghibta . . . surūri (Shaybi² 261, Massignon¹ M25, W 128)

The first three verses are also found in a manuscript in the Cairo Geniza.

Verse 1. "so my sadness was mixed with" (*fa-māzajat tarḥatī*): "and you became my joy and" (*wa-ṣirta farḥatī wa*), Massignon.

18. The Soul's Punishment in the Body's Prison

ḥawaytu bi-kullī . . . fī nafsī (Shaybi² 284, Massignon¹ M30, W 133)

As reported in *Akhbar* 38, Hallaj used these verses to publicly lament the unbearable treatment he had received from God.

Verse 1. "of your all" (*kullika*): "of your love" (*ḥubbika*), Massignon.

Verse 2. "I turn my heart" (*uqallibu qalbī*): This play on words alludes to a well-known hadith, "The heart of the believer is between two fingers of the Merciful, who turns it as he wishes" (see Schimmel, *Mystical Dimensions*, 197, 415). Here it signifies the overcoming or transformation of the heart by the object of its love, whether God or whatever is not God. This verse has a complicated double negative (literally, "I do not see anything except") followed by a tangled sequence of prepositions. The antithesis between "wildness" or "estrangement" (*waḥsha*) and "intimacy" (*uns*) is modulated with a twist; the author is estranged from what is not the beloved, and his intimacy is from the beloved— yet through what is other.

Verse 3. "affection" (*uns*): "humanity" (*ins*), Massignon.

"removed" (*mumanna'*): "hemmed round by" (*mujamma'*), Martin Lings, *Sufi Poems: A Mediaeval Anthology* (Cambridge, U.K.: Islamic Texts Society, 2004), no. 28.

19. Lovers' Perfection

idhā balagha al-ṣubbu . . . al-dhikr (Shaybi² 246, Massignon¹ M20, W 123)

Massignon's version proposes two recensions, rejected by Shaybi as misreadings. The first recension goes as follows:

When a youth reaches perfection in chivalry
    and gives up lover's union since he's drunk,
Then he attests sincerely what desire attests to him—
    that lovers' prayer is infidelity.

The second recension is basically the same as the text preferred by Shaybi, with the exception of the last line, which Massignon reads as "the knowers' prayer is infidelity." This version of the poem is sharply criticized by Ibn Taymiyya as heretical for its suggestion that obtaining union with God would make prayer superfluous.

20. Nearness and Distance Are One

fa-mā-lī . . . wāḥid (Shaybi[2] 229, Massignon[1] M13, W 116, *Tawasin* 6:12, ed. Nwyia, 205)

Ruzbihan comments on this passage, "Nearness and distance are one in unity for him who is not persecuted, and separation and union are one for him who is not rejected. And the one commanded to bow down to Adam, if he had prostrated, would have prostrated to God, with no other between" (*Mantiq al-asrar*, p. 160). Ruzbihan later added, "he saw otherness from the fact that he was veiled from the eternal by the temporal" (*Sharh-i shathiyyat*, 518).

Verse 1. "distance" (*bu`d*): "after" (*ba`d*), Shaybi.

Verse 2. "found" (*wājid*): "one" (*wāḥid*), Shaybi. Nuin/Janés translate *wājid* as "present."

21. Transcendence

juḥūdī fīka . . . tahwīs (Shaybi[2] 279, Massignon[1] M28–M29, W 131–32)

Transmitted by Qushayri in his Qur'an commentary, *Lata'if al-isharat* (on Qur'an 15:42), and by the noted nineteenth-century Baghdadian jurist Shihab al-Din al-Alusi. There is another version, which Massignon[1] treats as a separate poem (M29); the first and fourth verses of that are inserted in Ruzbihan's commentary on the *Tawasin* (on 6:9, ed. Massignon, p. 43; *Sharh-i shathiyyat*, 509; *Mantiq al-asrar*, p. 159). The same two verses, plus an additional line, are quoted by `Ayn al-Qudat Hamadani.

Verse 1. "my denial" (*juḥūdī*): "my madness" (*junūnī*).

"my thought" (*ẓannī*): "my reason" (*`aqlī*), Ruzbihan.

22. The Promise of Love

lya ḥabībun azūru . . . laḥẓāti (Shaybi[2] 214, Massignon[1] M11, W 114)

Quoted by al-Shattanawfi, al-Shushtari, and others.

Verse 1. "who visits" (*azūru*): A reading found in two manuscripts, preferable to "I visit" (*yazūru*), which would need an object.

Verse 2. "closely" (*bi-sirrī*, literally "with my conscience"), Shaybi: "with my hearing" (*bi-sam`ī*), Massignon.

Verse 3. "punctuation" (*nuqaṭ*), Shaybi: "voice" (*nuṭq*), Massignon.

23. Removing the Veil

yā shamsa yā badra . . . wa nāru (Shaybi[2] 263, Massignon[1] M26, W 129)

Also transmitted in the Cairo Geniza.

24. Voyager of Desire

mā ziltu aṭfuw . . . wa'nhaṭṭu (Shaybi[2] 297, Massignon[1] M34, W 137)

Quoted in the "Story of Husayn al-Hallaj" edited by Louis Massignon ("Qissat Husayn al-Hallâj," *Orientalia Suecana* 3 [1954], p. 17 of the Arabic text). Shaybi cites parallels in the poetry of Muslim ibn al-Walid Sari` al-Ghawani (d. 823) and others.

25. While Love Remains Secret

al-ḥubbu mā dāma . . . min al-ḥadhari (Shaybi[2] 259, Massignon[1] M24, W 127)

Shaybi compares this poem to the triumphal wine poems of Abu Nuwas, who extolled drinking publicly.

26. Veil of the Heart

badā laka sirrun . . . ẓalāmuhu (Shaybi[2] 484, Massignon[1] M52, W 156)

Quoted by Suhrawardi, the fifteenth-century Iranian philosopher Jalal al-Din al-Davani, the fourteenth-century Hanbali jurist Ibn Qayyim al-Jawziyya, and Ibn `Ajiba.

Shaybi considers this poem to be inauthentic and probably (including the three additional verses) by the prominent eleventh-century Andalusian Sufi Ibn al-`Arif. Massignon quotes the three additional verses from Ibn `Ajiba (*Iqāẓ*, 345), which can be translated as follows:

> For if you hid from it, then it would dwell in you, and you would stay
> on the side of the unveiling amidst its protected tents.
> Then comes a story that's never tiresome to hear,
> whose prose and poetry is enjoyable for us.
> If a soul mentions it, its fortune is blessed,
> and depression is removed from the afflicted heart.

Verse 1. "discover it" (*iktishāfuhu*), Wazin: "conceal it" (*iktitāmuhu*), Shaybi, Massignon, Ruspoli, i.e., "for a long time you concealed it."

27. Eyes of the Heart

fīka ma`nan yad`ū . . . ilayka (Shaybi[2] 397, Massignon[1] M43, W 146)

28. Burden of the Heart

ḥammaltum bil-qalb . . . al-budunu (Shaybi[2] 370, Massignon[1] M62, W 166)

Transmitted by Sulami in his Qur'an commentary *Haqa'iq al-tafsir* (on Qur'an 33:72).

29. Prison Letter

hammi bihi . . . ilayka (Shaybi[2] 392, Massignon[1] M44, W 147, Akhbar *2.)

From a letter to Hallaj's friend Ibn `Ata'. The third line resembles a line in poem 107, "I Am the One that I Desire."

Verse 1. "what touches you" (*yalīka*), Wazin: "praise of you" (*madḥatika*), Massignon.

30. In All Directions

raqībāni minnī shāhidāni . . . tarānī (Shaybi[2] 372, Massignon[1] M64, W 168)

Related by Ibn al-Jawzi (d. 1200), the famous Hanbali jurist and conservative Sufi.

Verse 1. "two" (*ithnān*), Massignon: "truly" (*annāni*), Shaybi, who sees an apparent mistake in the manuscript.

Verse 3. "sought the east" (*rumtu al-sharq*): "sought the market" (*rumtu al-sūq*), Akhuri.

Verse 6. "my tongue" (*lisānī*): "my heart" (*jinānī*), Massignon.

31. Something by My Heart

shay'un bi-qalbī . . . lā al-ẓulamu (Shaybi[2] 340, Massignon[1] M54, W 158)

Transmitted in Qushayri's Qur'an commentary.

Accepted by Shaybi[1] but later rejected by Shaybi[2]. He maintains that this was a "sensuous poem" that Hallaj wrote for a friend, but that he was incapable of departing from the mystical asceticism of his Sufi nature, so it became a mystical poem. Ruspoli (*Le Message de Hallâj l'Expatrié*, p. 287) prefers a variant of line 1 that alludes to a single name of God, which he argues should be *al-ḥaqq*, "the truth," according to the doctrine of Hallaj.

Verse 1. "there is something by my heart" (*shay'un bi-qalbī*): "your heart is something" (*qalbuka shay'un*), Massignon.

"names" (*asmā'*): "a name" (*ism*), Ruspoli.

32. Speech from the Beloved

khaṭabanī al-ḥaqqu . . . lisānī (Shaybi[2] 373, Massignon[1] M59, W 163)

Verse 2 is a typical example of using "tangled words" (using short prepositions and their antitheses): "He drew me near to him after I was distant" (*qarrabanī minhu ba`da bu`di*).

Shaybi[2] adds two more verses that are a pious qualification of the preceding declaration, which weakens it:

> I replied obediently when called,
>> responding to the one who called me.
> And I feared for how I sinned of old,
>> but my love secured my protection.

33. Hidden, Present

yā ghā'iban shāhidan . . . mawjūdu (Shaybi[2] 234, Massignon[1] M16b)

Massignon sees this as a statement of the "theory of the witness" in testament of beauty (*Passion* 3:25–27), translating the opening words as "O splendid witness, however You hide Yourself in Your invisibility."

Verse 1. "hidden, present" (*ghā'iban shāhidan*), Shaybi: "present, hidden," Massignon.

Verse 2. The key term here is "giving up" (*ṣabr `an*), normally recommended as discipline but yielding unfortunate results in love.

Verse 3. "heartsick" (*makmūd*), Shaybi: "rejected" (*majhūd*), Massignon.

34. I Wonder at You and Me

`ajibtu minka wa-minnī (Shaybi² 350, Massignon¹ Q9, W 94)

Quoted by Ruzbihan Baqli, Ibn Taymiyya, Sha`rani, Sarraj, Daylami, Ibn al-Dabbagh, and others, but only attributed to Hallaj by Shadhili and Manawi. The criticism comes from `Abd al-Wahhab al-Sha`rani, who nonetheless admires the verses.

Verse 3. "annihilated me" (*afnaytanī*): "enriched me" (*aghnaytanī*), certain MSS.

Verse 4. "my ease" (*ni`matī*): "my pleasure" (*nuzhatī*), certain MSS.

Verse 5. "whether," (*min ḥaythu*), Massignon: "since you are" (*idh kunta*), Wazin, following a MS.

35. I Found You by Sciences

innī wajadtuka . . . tazharu (Meier 63/138)

Verse 1. The second half of verse 1 appears to be lacking a syllable to fit the meter; this could be supplied by adding *wa-* before *tazharu*.

36. Open Secret

yā man yaṭūfu . . . al-khāfī (Meier 65/140)

37. Loss in Ecstasy Is Loss

ta'ammul al-wajdi . . . faqdu (Shaybi² 24, W 267)

This poem was rejected by Massignon¹, 149, but restored by Shaybi.

Verses 6–7. "I am counted" (*u`addu*), Wazin: "I multiply/enumerate" (*u`iddu*), Nuin/Janés. Shaybi does not vocalize this verb, leaving it ambiguous whether it is active or passive.

38. I Didn't Long

mā rumtu . . . al-dahshi (Meier 65/140)

39. Testament

a lā abligh aḥibbā'ī . . . al-safīna (Shaybi² 374, Massignon¹ M56, W 160)

Quoted by Qadi Hamid al-Din Nagawri (India, fourteenth century), in his commentary on the names of God, *Tawali` al-shumus.*

The quotation from al-Mursi that prefaces the poem continues, "It is as though he said, 'I will die upon the faith of Islam,' indicating that he would die crucified" (Shaybi¹, p. 308, quoting al-Sha`rani, *Lata'if al-minan* [Cairo: al-Matba`a al-Maymaniyya, 1321/1903], 2:84). Shaybi adds that the probable meaning of the verse is that Hallaj wanted to be the messiah of Sufism in surrender and self-sacrifice in order to establish its teaching—which he did.

Ruspoli (*Le Message de Hallâj l'Expatrié*, pp. 104–6) considers as a parallel the account of Moses and Khidr in sura 18 of the Qur'an, where Khidr indeed makes holes in ships to prevent their seizure by a tyrannical king; the analogy is inexact, however, since Hallaj's metaphorical ship has accomplished its voyage.

Ruspoli also questions Massignon's conventional translation of the place-names in the final phrase (*al-baṭḥā . . . al-madīna*) as Mecca and Medina, in light of the profound affection that Hallaj must have had for the holy cities, to which he had made pilgrimage three times. Ruspoli proposes, as a possible alternative, to read these terms generically as "the plain" and "the city," signifying Hallaj's rejection of both uninhabited nature and human civilization in his quest for annihilation. This abstraction seems far-fetched, since it evades the obvious antithesis between the symbols of Christian and Muslim religiosity.

Likewise, Ruspoli prefers to read the verb in the first verse as "He [God] wrecked" (*ankasara*) or "I [Hallaj] wrecked" (*ankasiru*) rather than as the impersonal "is wrecked" (*inkasara*), which is used somewhat irregularly with a feminine noun, but others such as Wazin consider this normal usage.

40. All of Me Becomes a Heart

idhā dhakartuka . . . awjaʿu (Shaybi[2] 300, Massignon[1] M36, W 139)

Quoted in *Bughyat al-wuʿat*, a work on the lives of grammarians, by the fifteenth-century Egyptian polymath al-Suyuti (who attributes it to the Iraqi grammarian Abu al-Barakat al-Anbari, d. 1181), also by the nineteenth-century Persian theologian Khwansari in his biographical dictionary *Rawdat al-jannat*, and in a mystical treatise by Ahmad al-Ghazali (the Sufi-minded brother of the famous theologian Abu Hamid al-Ghazali), the *Kitab al-tajrid*.

Verse 1. "kills" (*yaqtulu*): Massignon reads "bothers" (*yuqliqu*), which seems trivial. Shaybi[2] suggests "destroys" (*yutlifu*), but the reading "kills" (*yaqtulu*) is quoted by Ahmad al-Ghazali (*Kitāb al-tajrīd*). It seems a more appropriate contrast with sorrows and pains.

Verse 2. "calling" (*dāʿiya*): "attentive" (*wāʿiya*), Ghazali, in Shaybi.

Verse 3. An additional verse is introduced by Shaybi, though it appears banal: "If I spoke, I am all tongues about you, / and if I heard, I am all ears for you."

41. Blameless

lā talumnī fal-lawm . . . wāḥidu (Shaybi[2] 230, Massignon[1] M14, W 117, *Tawasin* 6:29, ed. Nwyia, 209)

Verse 2. "I am true to your true promise" (*anā fī waʿdika al-ḥaqqi ḥaqqu*), Nwyia: "Within your promise, your true promise, is a truth" (*inna fil-waʿdi waʿdika al-ḥaqq haqqa*), Massignon, Shaybi.

Verse 3. "Whoever wants speech—here's my writing" (*man arāda al-khiṭāba hādhā kitābī*), Nwyia: "Whoever wants writing—here's my speech" (*man arāda al-kitāb hādhā khiṭābī*), Massignon, Shaybi (an illogical formulation, since speech cannot be read).

42. Dyed in Blood

lā tuʿarriḍ . . . al-ʿushshāqi (Shaybi[2] 474, Massignon[1] Y7)

Transmitted by Abu Bakr ibn Yazdanyar (author of an important tenth-century treatise on Sufism), Ghazali, Subki.

43. My Drinking Buddy

nadīmī ghayru . . . min al-ḥayfi (Shaybi² 466, Massignon¹ M37, W 140)

Quoted by al-Sulami in his *tafsir* (commentary on Qur'an 42:17), Qushayri in his tafsir (commentary on Qur'an 28:30), al-Raghib, Ibn al-Jawzi, Baqli in his tafsir (commentary on Qur'an 7:155), `Attar, al-Qaysari, al-Sha`rawi, al-Minawi, Ibn `Arabi, and many more. Others such as al-Tha`alibi attribute the poem to al-Husayn ibn al-Dahhak or Abu Nuwas. Shaybi rejects it altogether.

The last line has obscure readings; while Massignon prefers *tinnīn* (Leo, or "dragon," the constellation of Draco), Shaybi makes a good case for *nasrayn* (the two stars Sirius and Procyon, known collectively as the "dog stars," who rule over the late summertime, the "dog days," when trouble is likely to occur). In any case, this reads as a grim prophecy of Hallaj's martyrdom. Farid al-Din `Attar memorably translated it into Persian verse.

44. Kill Me, Friends

uqtulūnī . . . mamātī (Shaybi² 204, Massignon¹ Q10, W 96)

One of the most widely cited poems of Hallaj, this is quoted by the philosopher Suhrawardi, Ibn `Arabi, the geographer Qazwini (d. 1283) in his *Wonders of Creation* (`Aja'ib al-makhluqat*), `Izz al-Din Maqdisi, Simnani, Jildaki, `Ali al-Qari, and many more.

Several later authors, including Sadr al-Din al-Qunawi (d. 1273),the Sufi metaphysician, and `Abd al-Qadir al-Jazai'iri (d. 1882), the hero of Algerian resistance against the French, wrote responses to this poem, directed to the riddling middle section. Rumi responded to it in two Persian ghazals (*Diwan*, 2813, also 386).

Massignon maintains that this poem consists of three parts: the first eight verses are a prediction of the execution of Hallaj and the miracle of the ashes, the second part is a riddle about "the paternity of the Holy Spirit" (!), and the last section concerns the alchemical magnum opus. He regards the first and third parts as "possibly authentic." The first two verses echo an early profane Arabic poem by Mu'ammal ibn Jamil.

Verse 19. This verse contains an unreproducible play on words (*bi-jiwārin sāqiyāti wa-siwāqin jāriyāti*) that deploys two different roots symmetrically in identical grammatical patterns.

45. Punishment

urīduka lā urīduka . . . `iqābi (Shaybi² 412, Massignon¹ M7, W 109)

This poem is rejected by al-Shaybi and Ruspoli; Sirjani (p. 89) attributes it to Ibn `Ata'.

Verse 1. "I want you" (*urīduka*): "I love you" (*uḥibbuka*) in Ibn al-Dabbagh and Ibn Qayyim.

"the penalty" is taken in the sense of "my penalty" in Ibn `Arabi and Qaysari.

46. Sacrifice

inna al-ḥabība . . . lil-ḥarami (Shaybi² 487, Massignon¹ M51, W 154)

Quoted by Ibn `Arabi (anonymously), the Moroccan hagiographer al-Tadili (d. 1230), and the Egyptian biographer of Sufis al-Yafi`i (d. 1367).

Massignon only presents three verses, corresponding to verses 4, 7, and 5 of Shaybi's version. Massignon questions how Hallaj could have written this intense poem on the hajj, when as we know he recommended a substitute ritual in which one makes a small model of the Ka`ba in one's house.

47. Infidel

kafartu . . . qabīḥu (Shaybi[2] 225, Massignon[1] Y2)

Transmitted by `Ayn al-Qudat, Sari `Abd Allah, Ibn `Arabi.

Verse 1. "detestable" (*qabīḥ*): Shaybi records the variant "forbidden" (*ḥarām*) from a manuscript owned by Muhammad Alwan.

48. The Fate of the Arrogant

qad kuntu . . . al-baṭari (Shaybi[2] 267, Massignon[1] Y4)

Transmitted by Sulami in his tafsir on Qur'an 39:39. Massignon attributes it to Abu al-Atahiya (but the reference is unsupported).

49. You've Watched Me

*ra`aytanī . . . wabiyya* (Shaybi[2] 399, Ta`arruf 1659–61)

Quoted by Kalabadhi only as by "one of the great ones."

Verse 3. "goes by night" (*asrā*), see Quran 17:1, an allusion to the night journey (*isrā'*) and ascension (*mi`rāj*) of the Prophet Muhammad.

50. The Thread of Desire

sa-ajma`u ghazla . . . kulla fann (Meier 64/139)

51. Cramped

`ajibtu li-kullī . . . arḍī (Shaybi[2] 296, Massignon[1] M33, W 136)

Also transmitted by `Izz al-Din Maqdisi.

52. Illumination

`aqd al-nubuwwati . . . ta'mūrī (Shaybi[2] 235, Massignon[1] M21, W 124)

This poem comments on the Qur'an's "light verse" (Qur'an 24:35), which describes the light of God as a lamp (*miṣbāḥ*) guarded in a niche (*mishkāt*, translated here as "chamber"), whose light glows with an immortal light. Hallaj's preoccupation with Moses is explored in more detail in the *Tawasin*.

Verse 3. "my spirit" (*rūḥī*), a reading restored by Shaybi from a manuscript: "my condition" (*ṭūrī*) or "my nature," Nuin/Janés.

53. God's Explanation

bayānu bayāni al-ḥaqqi . . . lisānuhu (Shaybi[2] 373, Massignon[1] M63, W 167)

Shaybi mistakenly observes that the second and third verses of this poem are quoted in one manuscript of Ruzbihan's *Sharh-i shathiyyat*, but not in the printed edition. In fact, the text contains (p. 389) a superior reading of verses 2 through 4, confirmed by *Mantiq al-asrar*, p. 123. Verse 3 echoes a saying (or hadith) that "One who knows God, his tongue is stilled" (*kalla lisānuhu*). See Muhammad `Ali Tahanawi, *Mawsu`at kashshaf istilahat al-funun wal-`ulum*, ed. Rafiq al-`Ajam (Beirut: Librarie du Liban, 1996), p. 1585a.

Verse 2. "I pointed" (*ashirtu*), Ruzbihan, clearly indicated in the Persian translation: "you pointed" (*ashirta*), Shaybi.

Verse 3. "is astonished" (*taḥayyara*), Ruzbihan: "you point" (*tushīru*), Shaybi.

"message" (*adhān*), Ruzbihan: "times" (*awān*), Shaybi.

54. Knower of the Revelation

ḥaqīqat al-ḥaqq mustanīr . . . khabīr (Shaybi² 265, Massignon¹ M17, W 120)

Quoted by Sulami in his tafsir on Qur'an 10:35.

Verse 1. "a cry" (*ṣārikhatan*): "can produce a cry of alarm" (*ṣārikhuhu*), Massignon; compare Qur'an 36:43, *ṣarīkh*, "cry for help."

"Knower" (*khabīr*) is one of the ninety-nine names of God, though Massignon translates this as "the foretelling of a sure event."

Verse 2. "a reality [in which]" (*ḥaqīqatun fīhi*), Shaybi: "it's the reality of Truth" (*ḥaqīqat al-ḥaqq*), Wazin; "realities" (*ḥaqā'iq*), Sulami in *Essai*, p. 373, no. 61.

"Goal" (*matlab*): "result" (*mablagh*), Sulami.

55. Temple and Light

haykalī al-jism . . . `alīm (Shaybi² 332, Massignon¹ M53, W 157)

Shaybi interprets this as an anthropology describing first the elemental and material human body, then the luminous divinity. The adjectives employed at the end of the first verse combine epithets restricted exclusively to God ("eternity," *ṣamad*) and to humanity ("devout," *dayyān*). One of Shaybi's colleagues, Dr. Ibrahim Basyuni, has commented on the similarity of this verse to Taoist poetry (Shaybi², 332).

Verse 1. "spirit" (*rūḥ*): "essence" (*dhāt*) in some MSS.

56. Reason's Ears and Eyes

li-anwāri nūri 'l-dīni . . . asrāru (Shaybi² 240, Massignon¹ M22, W 125)

Verse 1. "light" (*nūr*) (*Akhbār* 33): "religion" (*dīn*), Shaybi, Massignon.

57. How Often Were We Hidden

yā ṭālamā ghibnā . . . al-qamar (Shaybi² 254, Massignon¹ Q11, W 98)

The transmitter, al-Jawbari, describes these verses as part of a longer poem by Hallaj on the secret of invisibility (with only three verses, however, it can hardly be evaluated as an example of the *qasida*). See 'Abd al-Rahmâne al-Djawbarî, *Le Voile arraché: l'autre visage de l'Islam*, trans. René R. Khawam (Paris: Phébus, 1979), 1:57–59.

58. Ecstasies and States

mawājīdu ḥaqqin . . . akābiri (Shaybi[2] 249, Massignon[1] M19, W 122)

59. What Wonderful Relief

ni`ma al-i`ānatu . . . khalalih (Shaybi[2] 328, Massignon[1] M48, W 151, Meier 66/142)

Found in the Cairo Geniza. The Shiraz manuscript described by Meier preserves a longer version than Massignon had (with the addition of a final fifth verse), but the former text is in part confusing and illegible. The version here follows Shaybi but adds Meier's fifth verse.

Verse 1. "What wonderful relief" (*ni`ma al-i`āna*): "the nature of liberation" (*na`t al-ighāthati*), Meier; "gifts of" (*ni`am*), Ruspoli, who reads the meter as *tawil* instead of *basit*.

"Grace" (*luṭufin*): "of his grace" (*luṭfihi*), Ruspoli.

"Clouds" (*khalal*), Shaybi and Wazin, literally, the gaps between clouds from which rain falls: "qualities" (*khilal*), Massignon.

Verse 2. "just so" (*ṭawran*): *ṭūran* ("a Sinai"), Massignon[2].

"from his mountains he would veil my brothers" (*fa-yaghshā `alā al-ikhwāni min qulalihi*), Massignon: "I gather ecstasies from his mountain peaks" (*min shāhiqin ujtanī al-aḥwāla*), Meier.

Massignon's initial translation of verse 2 was straightforward: "Sometimes He regards me, and sometimes I regard Him, He who, if he wishes, rains down (like a storm) from above on the mountains, on our friends" (Massignon[1]). In his revised translation, Massignon cited the depiction of a mountain storm in Qur'an 24:43: "Sometimes this grace makes me into a Sinai, from which I regard him above, I who am showered with what falls on the mountains" (Massignon[2]).

Ruspoli argues instead that the verb *yaghsha* ("veils") refers to the vision of Qur'an 53:16, the veiling or shrouding of the lotus tree of paradise, so the verse would read, "if God deigns, he would cover the brethren with his effusions" (*Le Message de Hallâj l'Expatrié*, 263). Nuin and Janés translate this as "If he wishes, from his height he would pounce upon the brothers" (Mansur Hallay, *Diván* [Madrid: Ediciones del Oriente y del Mediterráneo, 2002], 167).

Verse 3. "his waters" (*balalihi*), Meier: "his religions" (*milalihi*), Shaybi.

Verse 4. "sees . . . me" (*yashhadunī*), Meier: "sees . . . it" (*yashhaduhu*), Shaybi and Wazin.

"his romantic character" (*al-shakhṣ min ṭalalihi*), i.e., a person from the picturesque ruin that figures in the opening of many an Arabic poem.

60. Riding on Reality

rukūbu 'l-ḥaqīqati . . . tadiqq (Shaybi[2] 310, Massignon[1] M40, W 143)

Found in the Geniza. Most interpreters make the metaphor of "riding" into an abstraction ("joining"), but the logic of the poem requires a more physical image, a point acknowledged in the Persian translation of this poem by Akhuri.

Verse 2. "nonexistence" (*faqd al-wujūd*): "the source of existence" (`*ayn al-wujūd*), Massignon.

61. The Conscience and the Path

ṣayyaranī al-ḥaqqu . . . wal-wathīqa (Shaybi[2] 318, Massignon[1] M38, W 141, *Tawasin* 3:11, ed. Nwyia, 197; Ruzbihan, *Mantiq al-asrar*, p. 124)

Verse 1. "the 'H' of reality" (*hā' ḥaqīqatih*), *Tawasin* 3:11, Ruzbihan; "by reality" (*bil-ḥaqīqa*), Massignon.

Verse 2. "and that one" (*wa-dhā*): "beyond" (*warā'*), Ruzbihan. "What witness now (in me) is my subconsciousness, without my (created) personality" (Massignon). Wazin's reading (*shāhida*, "as the witness," in place of *shāhada*, "which witnessed") connects the two lines grammatically, so that the "witness" is what the Truth (*al-haqq*) has made the speaker become.

62. The Secret of Mysteries

sirru 'l-sarā'iri . . . bi-ṭiyyāti (Shaybi[2] 212, Massignon[1] M12, W 115)

Transmitted by Nabulsi. For the Muslim profession of faith, see A. J. Wensinck and A. Rippin, "Tashahhud," in *Encyclopaedia of Islam, Second Edition*, ed. P. Bearman, Th. Bianquis, C. E. Bosworth, E. van Donzel, and W. P. Heinrichs, consulted online on December 24, 2017, http://dx.doi.org.libproxy.lib.unc.edu/10.1163/1573-3912_islam_SIM_7427. For the formula "without asking how," associated with the school of al-Ash`ari, see W. Montgomery Watt, "Ash`ariyya", in ibid., consulted online on December 24, 2017, http://dx.doi.org.libproxy.lib.unc.edu/10.1163/1573-3912_islam_COM_0067.

63. I've Thought about Religions

tafakkartu fil-adyāni . . . jamma (Shaybi[2] 335, Massignon[1] M50, W 153)

64. Name and Meaning

ismun ma`a . . . ma`ānīhi (Shaybi[2] 391, Massignon[1] M69, W 173)

Massignon entitles this poem "Against the Superstition of the 'Greatest Name.'"

Verse 2. "revealed it" (*yabdīhi*), Massignon, Wazin: "is its Creator" (*mubdiyahu*), Massignon[1], p. 168.

65. Near and Far

fa-qultu akhillā'i . . . bu`du (Shaybi[2] 435, Massignon[1] Y3)

66. Intimacy with God

wujūduhu bī . . . wāṣifu (Shaybi[2] 304, W 275)

67. Vanishing Ascension

samawtu sumuwwan . . . al-wajdi (Meier 65/141)

There is a complex wordplay here between "existence" (*wujūd*), and "ecstasy" or "finding" (alternative meanings of *wajd*).

68. I Have Control of Things

uṣarrafu fil-ashyā' . . . *uṣarrafu* (Meier 64/139)

69. Consider My Apparition

ta'ammul khayālī . . . *aḍwā* (Meier 63/138)

70. Love Is in Primordial Eternity

al-ʿishqu fi azal al-āzāl . . . *ibdā'u* (Shaybi² 177, Massignon² Q8b, W 99)

This is the poem that inspired the title of al-Daylami's treatise *The Book of the Inclination of the Affectionate Alif towards the Inclined Lam*, translated by Joseph Norment Bell and Hassan Mahmood Abdul Latif Al Shafie as *A Treatise on Mystical Love*, where the poem is quoted on p. 71. Hallaj's prose discourse on love is translated in ibid., pp. 40–43. The poem is convincingly analyzed by Nasrollah Pourjavady in *Kirishma-i ʿishq: maqalati dar ʿirfan-i naw-Hallaji-i Iran* [*The glittering of love: Essays on Neo-Hallājian, mysticism in Iran*] (Tehran: Farhang-i Nashr-i Naw, 1393/2015), pp. 19–36. While Massignon argues that the letters were *alif-lam* as the definite article, and Shaybi sees them as symbolic of the spirit, Pourjavady points out the lack of evidence for those theories. He argues that *lam-alif* is in the theophanic "glittering" (*talā'lā'a*) described in this poem, establishing a major theme that later poets like Ahmad Ghazali adopted.

Verse 2. "whose martyrs are alive" (*li-man qutlāhu aḥyā'u*), an obvious reference to Qur'an 2:154, "Do not call them dead who are killed on the path of God; rather, they are alive (*aḥyā'un*) though you are not aware." This plural noun is the subject of the verbs in verses 7 and 8, providing a symmetrical structure.

71. Which Earth Lacks You?

wa-ayyu 'l-arḍi . . . *samā'u* (Shaybi² 175, Massignon¹ M1, W 103)

Transmitted by the fourteenth-century scholar al-Firkawi, in his commentary on the treatise on the spiritual path by ʿAbd Allah al-Ansari, *Manazil al-sa'irin.*

72. Beware Consolation

ʿalayka ya nafsu . . . *wal-takhallī* (Shaybi² 392, Massignon¹ M46, W 149)

Verse 1. "for power" (*fal-ʿizz*), Wazin: "power" (*al-ʿizz*), Massignon.

73. This World Deceives Me

dunyā tukhādiʿunī . . . *ḥālaha* (Shaybi² 325, Massignon¹ M45, W 148)

A popular poem, this is quoted in Qazwini's *ʿAja'ib*, al-Raghib al-Isfahani, Ibn Fadl Allah, al-Khatib al-Baghdadi, Ahmad al-Rifaʿi, Abu al-ʿAbbas al-Shurayshi's commentary on the rhyming tales of al-Hariri (*Sharh al-maqamat al-haririyya*), and Ibn Kathir's history *al-Bidaya wal-nihaya*. This poem is also attributed to ʿAli ibn Abi Talib.

Verse 2. "outlawed" (*ḥaẓura*), Wazin: "condemned" (*dhamma*), Massignon; "forbade" (*manaʿa*), Shurayshi.

"God" (*al-ilāh*): "the owner" (*al-malīk*), al-Khatib.

74. The Steeds of Separation

idhā dahamatka . . . al-rajā' (Shaybi² 171, Massignon¹ M4, W 106)

75. Pilgrim's Prayer

labbayka labbayka . . . ma`nā'ī (Shaybi² 182, Massignon¹ Q1, W 79)

Found in the Geniza and in Ibn al-Jawzi, Baha' al-Din al-`Amuli, and Nabulsi.

On this poem, Hujwiri (who quotes verses 1, 3, and 4) makes the following comment:

> God divided the one substance of His love and bestows a particle thereof, as a peculiar gift, upon every one of His friends in proportion to their enravishment with Him; then He lets down upon the particle the shrouds of humanity and nature and temperament in spirit, in order that by its powerful working it may transmute to its own quality all the particles that are attached to it, until the lover's clay is wholly converted into love, and all his actions and looks become so many indispensable conditions of love. This stage is named "union" alike by those who regard the inward meaning and those who regard the outward expression. (*Kashf al-mahjub*, ed. Zhukovsky, p. 332; trans. Nicholson, *Revealing the Mystery*, pp. 258–59)

Verse 2. "whispered" (*nājaytu*), Massignon: "called" (*nādaytu*), Wazin.

Verse 3. "gesture" (*īmā'*), Wazin: "vision" (*i`yā'*), Massignon.

76. How Long Do You Contest

ilā kam anta . . . la tarāhu (Shaybi² 168, Massignon¹ M2, W 104)

A conventional sermon; Massignon did not bother to translate it in his first edition, regarding it as a late production, probably by Hurayfish Makki (d. 1398). Shaybi considers it as likely by Abu al-Atahiyya.

77. Intellect's Advice

man rāma . . . talhū (Shaybi² 388, Massignon¹ M66, W 170, *Ta`arruf* 730)

Transmitted by the famous Naqshbandi Sufi of Herat, `Abd al-Rahman Jami (d. 1492), in *Naqd al-nusus*, his commentary on ibn `Arabi's abridged version of *Fusus al-hikam*.

Verse 2. "deception" (*talbīs*): "fraud" (*tadlīs*), Shaybi.

78. Song of Death

an`ā ilayka . . . al-qidami (Shaybi² 495, Massignon¹ Q6, W 88)

Massignon asserts, "This text is the key for understanding the whole of Hallaj's thought" (*Passion*, 1:573). Sarraj (*Kitab al-luma`*, p. 248) attributes this poem to Nuri as recited by Qannad, and calls it a description of "the destruction of his spiritual state" (*faqd ḥālihi*).

Verse 1. "went astray" (*ṭāḥa*): Wazin glosses this as "is destroyed, disappears" (*halaka, saqaṭa*).

Verse 8. "dumber" (*a`yā*), Wazin: "blinder" (*a`mā*), Massignon.

79. Guidance of the Lost

yā jāhilan . . . mawqifu (Shaybi² 305; W 276)

80. There Are Four Letters

ahruf arba'a bi-hā hāma . . . wa-fikrī (Shaybi² 263, Massignon¹ M27, W 130)

The letters that provide the answer to this riddle form an irregular acrostic. *A* is for *tA'lafu*, *L* for *maLāma*, *L* for *aL-ma'ānī*, *H* for *uHīmu* (the second *A* is technically not written); thus is "Allah" formed.

Quoted by Ibn 'Ata' Allah, 'Ali al-Burhani, Jumayli, Ibn 'Ajiba, and Sulami.

Verse 2. "to creation" (*bil-ṣun'i*), Shaybi²: "to shedding [blood/tears]," *bi-ṣafḥi*), Shaybi³.

Verse 3. "can you guess?" (*a tadrī*): "by which I know" (*wa-adrī*), Shaybi, Wazin.

81. Three Letters without Dots

thalāthatu ahrufi . . . kalāmu (Shaybi² 334, Massignon¹ M49, W 152)

The first line is quoted in the theological encyclopedia of al-Baghdadi, *al-Farq bayn al-firaq*, as Hallaj's reply when asked about his sins (chapter 4, part 10, on the incarnationists or *hulūliyya*).

The first dotted letter *T* is used grammatically for the second person, hence those lovers who are in ecstasy from hearing God's address to them. The second dotted letter *Y* is also the first-person singular suffix meaning "my" (Arabic *-i*), which everyone uses for self-affirmation. The three remaining undotted letters (*W-Ḥ-D*) are the root for unity, which is unattainable.

Ruspoli (*Le Message de Hallâj l'Expatrié*, p. 290) maintains instead that the answer to the riddle is the divine name *al-ḥaqq*, "the Truth." He sees the three undotted letters as *A*, *L*, *Ḥ*, the two dotted letters as the repeated *Q*, and the three remaining letters as the letters that spell "Allah."

Verse 2. "resembles his ecstatic lovers" (*yushākilu wājidīhi*): "indicates each ecstasy" (Massignon, *Passion* 1:287), though the explanation is unclear (ibid., 1:287, n. 78).

Verse 3. "a ciphered riddle" (*marmūzun mu'amma*), Massignon: "an excused cipher" (*marmūzun mu'āfī*), several MSS.

"for there is no travel here" (*fa-lā safarun hunāka*), Wazin: "and no travel reaches it" (*fa-lā safarun yunālu*), Massignon.

82. You Who Are Unaware

yā ghāfilan li-jahālati . . . wa-bayānī (Shaybi² 358, Massignon¹ M58, W 162)

This riddle has produced some surprisingly different answers. Massignon argues that the first answer is "my law" (*nāmūsī*, from the Greek *nomos*), which is then altered into the phrase "I am Moses" (*anā mūsá*) by prefixing the letter *alif*. The two dotted letters are *nūn* and *yā'*.

With a technically more developed lexical argument, Shaybi¹ (p. 293) proposes instead the word "unification" (*ittiḥād*), or union with God, which he sees as the goal of the

Sufi's worship. The two dotted letters are the two repetitions of *tā'*, the first of which is a regular transformation of the first letter of the root *W-Ḥ-D*, while the second *tā'* is a feature of the eighth verbal form; thus the first *tā'* is "a root."

Ruspoli (*Le Message de Hallâj l'Expatrié*, no. 71, p. 288) sees this rather as a reference to the Qur'anic phrase spoken by God—"I am I, your Lord" (*innī anā rabbuka*)—that is associated with the theophany of Mount Sinai, where the repeated letter *nūn* constitutes the two dotted letters. He is forced, however, to entertain two possibilities to fit the six letters specified by the riddle: "I am I" (*innī anā*) and "I am your Lord" (*anā rabbuka*).

Massignon's reading is most convincing. It has both depth and boldness, and it successfully recalls the decisive ambiguity of poem 52, "Illumination," where Moses and Hallaj fade in and out of the spot where revelation is received.

83. Return to God

irja` ilā allāh . . . illā hū (Shaybi[2] 386, Massignon[1] M65, W 169)

This riddle focuses on the word spelled by the two letters *mīm* and *`ayn*, which form *ma`a* or "with." This simple preposition conjoins God and creation; their relationship in effect makes the creation sacred. Thus the Muslim confession of divine unity ("there is no God but He") paradoxically entails the sanctification of creation, which is "with God." In verse 3, the one who unties the knot is the speaker of the poem, who is decoding the meaning of "with" from its spelling for the benefit of people who only know how to recite the creed. The Master of verse 4 is Muhammad, whose role is spelled out in the second half of the Muslim confession of faith ("Muhammad is the messenger of God"); yet here, he is not merely a prophetic representative but one who has attained union ("This is He!"). This recalls a prophetic saying that prominently features the word "with": "I have a time with God [*lī ma`a allāhi waqtun*] in which no close angel or deputed prophet is permitted alongside me" (see the index to hadith sayings quoted by Rumi, Badi` al-Zaman Furuzanfarr, *Aḥadith-i mathnawī* [Tehran: Danishgah-i Tihran, 1335], p. 39).

Although there is nothing in the context or the text itself to suggest an Isma`ili interpretation, Massignon could not resist linking the letters *mīm* and *`ayn* to the arcane sectarian views of the Shi`i groups known as the Mimiyya and the `Ayniyya, who variously hold the spiritual supremacy of either Muhammad or `Ali; further, he detects a reference to the Siniyya partisans of the supremacy of Salman the Persian in the final letter *S* (*sīn*) in the word "to sanctify" (*taqdīs*). For details, focusing on these figures as seen by modern Nusayris or Alawites, see Matti Moosa, *The Extremist Shiites: The Ghulat Sects* (Syracuse, N.Y.: Syracuse University Press, 1988), pp. 342–51. Ruspoli, in contrast, sees in the letter *`ayn* an allusion to Jesus (`Īsā).

Verse 1. "when you've reached the end, there is no God" (*fa-lā ilāha idhā bālaghta*): "there is no 'why' in the hereafter" (*wa-lā li-mādhā bil-ghayb*), *Passion* 1:290, a variant that Massignon previously rejected.

Verse 2. "is *with*" (*la-ma`a*): "is the light of" (*lama`a*), Nuin/Janés.

Verse 3. "knot" (*mun`aqadan*), Shaybi: "belief" (*mu`taqadan*), Massignon.

Verse 5. "is shown" (*yuftaḥu*): Technically, this can mean "is vocalized with A," once again yielding *ma`a* (*Akhbar*, p. 134, n. 5).

84. Suggestion and Expression

katabtu ilayhi . . . al-ishāra (Shaybi² 274, W 273)

85. Silence

sukūtun thumma ṣamt . . . ramsu (Shaybi² 277, Massignon¹ Q4, W 57)

Quoted by Yafi`i and the eminent late-Ottoman Sufi scholar Ahmad Gumushkhanevi (d. 1894).

Verse 6 of Massignon is omitted by Shaybi:

> And rapture, then repelling, then attraction;
> and description, then unveiling, then investiture.

86. You're the Viewpoint

yā mawḍi` al-nāẓir . . . khāṭirī (Shaybi² 244, Massignon¹ Q3, W 83)

Quoted by Ruzbihan Baqli, Jildaki, Ibn al-Khatib.

Ruzbihan explains the origin of this poem as a response by Hallaj to Shibli: "In an allusion to 'essential union,' he said in conversation with Shibli, 'God created hearts, and inside them he placed his secret. He created breaths, and he made their flow from inside the heart, between the secret and the heart; he placed knowledge in the heart and unity in the secret. Not a breath exhales without allusion to unity and proof of knowledge in the extension of disturbance by the world of lordship. Every breath that is devoid of this is dead, and its owner is responsible for that.' Then in this influence he recited these verses . . ." (*Sharh-i shathiyyat*, p. 381).

The repetition in verse 5 of *yasrī . . . tasrī*, "steals forth . . . steals forward," also evokes the *isrā'* or night journey that was the preliminary to the Prophet Muhammad's ascension to paradise.

87. The Condition of Knowledge

sharṭ al-ma`ārifi . . . muṭṭali`u (Massignon¹ Y5, *Ta`arruf* 1685)

88. Dualities

lil-`ilmi ahlun . . . tajārību (Shaybi² 194, Massignon¹ Q2, W 81)

Verse 6. "was afraid" (*minhu mar`ūb*), Shaybi: "kept its taste" (*minhu marghūb*), Massignon, *Passion* 3:338.

Verse 9. "didn't touch it" (*mā massahu*), Wazin: "has been drenched with it" ([*mā*] *māssahu*), Massignon.

Verse 13. "darkening" (*ghirbīb*): a rare term from the verbal root *gharaba*, which relates to the setting of the sun, and the similar form *gharābīb* (found in Qur'an 35:27) denotes a black color, like that of the crow or raven (*ghurāb*).

89. The Wings of My Intention

ashāra laḥẓī . . . wahmi (Shaybi² 338, Massignon¹ Q7, W 90)

Verse 7. "book" (*sijillin*, meaning a document or registry), Shaybi, Wazin, a metaphor for the heavenly tablets inscribed with the destinies of humans: "vessels of water" (*sijālin*), an apparent mistake by Massignon, translated as "mirror of water"; "my consciousness" (*ḍamīrī*), another MS.

Verse 8. "rope" (*ḥabla*), Shaybi, Wazin: "end" (*ḥadda*), Massignon.

90. Keeping the Secret

man sārarūhu . . . ghashshāsha (Shaybi[2] 286, Massignon[1] Q5, W 86)

Quoted by al-Sulami, Ibn al-Jawzi, Hujwiri, Ibn al-Saʿi, Ruzbihan Baqli (tafsir on Qurʾan 16:46), Ibn ʿArabi, ʿIzz al-Din Maqdisi, and many more.

Verse 1. "all that they concealed" (*kullamā satarū*): "the secret publicly" (*al-sirra mushtahiran*), Baqlī, tafsir on Qurʾan 16:47; "the secret judiciously" (*al-sirra mujtahidan*), Ibn ʿArabi, *Futūḥāt*.

Verse 2. "acquired" (*ḥamalat*): "ignored" (*khamalat*), Massignon.

Verse 5. "they avoid him, for he's not fit for their company" (*wa-jānibūhu fa-lam yaṣluḥ bi-qurbihim*): "He came in splendor, and did not enjoy their company" (*wa-jāʾa bi-nawhin fa-lam yasʿad bi-qurbihim*), Baqlī.

Verse 9. "a revealer of" (*mudhīʿan baʿḍa*), Wazin: "a guest, from jealousy" (*muḍīfan baghḍa*), Massignon

"their majesty" (*jalālahum*): "their affection" (*wadādahum*), Baqli.

91. The Claim of Poverty

zaʿamta bil-faqri . . . marāmīhi (Meier 66/141)

92. The Secrets of Truth

sarāʾir al-ḥaqq . . . li-mukhfīhi (Shaybi[2] 398)

Quoted anonymously by Kalabadhi (*Taʿarruf* 1566), this poem is accepted by Shaybi but not by others.

Verse 2. "and then you claim him" (*fa-tūfīhi*): "and you get exhausted," Nuin/Janés; "and then you shelter there" (*fa-tuʾwīhi*), a variant in Kalabadhi, though the Persian gloss is "so that you seize him by your hand" (*tā ū-rā bi-dast ārī*).

93. He Opened the Veil

abdā al-ḥijāba . . . yaḥḍuru (Shaybi[2] 271, W 269, *Taʿarruf* 1458–63)

Verse 1. "imagined" (*yakhṭuru*), Wazin: "present" (*yaḥḍuru*), *Taʿarruf*.

Verse 2. "in ecstasy" (*mā al-wujūd*), Shaybi[2]: "by existence" (*bil-wujūd*), *Taʿarruf*.

94. Drunk and Sober

kafāka . . . ajdaru (Shaybi[2] 272, W 270, *Taʿarruf* 1498)

On intoxication (*sukr*) and sobriety (*ṣaḥw*), see *Words of Ecstasy*, pp. 49–50.

Verse 1. "sobriety revealed you" (*al-ṣaḥwa awjada annatī*, the last word anomalous but glossed in Persian as "your existence becomes apparent in you," *hastī-i tū dar tū padīd mī-āyad*), *Ta`arruf*: "drunkenness found my sorrow" (*al-sukra awjada kurbatī*), Shaybi; "found" (*awjada*): "increased," Nuin/Janés.

95. Jealousy of God

law shi'tu kashshaftu . . . bi-asrāri (Shaybi² 273, W 272)

96. Total Fusion

a-yā mawlāya . . . wal-tasallī (Shaybi² 331, W 280)

Verse 2. "You've already revealed" (*awḍaḥta*): "I've revealed" (*awḍaḥtu*), Wazin.

"showing them" (*bi-`arḍikahā*): "by your showing" (*bi-`arḍikum*), Nuin/Janés.

97. Vision of the End

idhā waswasat . . . wal-kursī (Massignon¹ Y8; Ruzbihan, *Manṭiq al-asrār*, p. 123; *Sharḥ-i shaṭḥiyyāt*, p. 421, no. 758).

98. Is It You or I?

a anā am anta? . . . ithnayni (Shaybi² 364, Massignon¹ M55, W 159)

Quoted by `Ayn al-Qudat, Ruzbihan, Anqarawi, Sari `Abd Allah, Nabulsi, Najm Razi, Nasir al-Din Tusi, `Afif al-Din Tilimsani, Rashid al-Din Fazl Allah, Da'ud al-Qaysari, Dihdar Fani, Sadr al-Din Shirazi, al-Gumushkhanevi, Suhrawardi, and Khwansari.

This poem is distinguished by a markedly philosophical vocabulary, featuring abstractions based on grammatical particles: "he-ness" (*huwiyya*), "nothingness" (*lā'iyya*), and "that-ness" or the "I am" (*al-inniyyu*), the latter often merging with "I-ness" (*anāniyya*).

99. His Memory Is Mine

dhikruhu . . . ma`a (Shaybi² 302, Massignon¹ Y6, *Tawasin* 6:15, ed. Nwyia, 206)

100. Mixing Spirits

jubbilat rūḥuka . . . al-fatiq (Shaybi² 307, Massignon¹ M41, W 144)

Transmitted by al-Khatib al-Baghdadi, the Mamluk literary scholar Jamal al-Din al-Watwat (d. 1318), and Ibn Kathir. Sirjani (p. 181) attributes this poem to Abu `Ali al-Mawsili.

101. I Wrote You

katabtu wa-lam aktub . . . kitābi (Shaybi² 192, Massignon¹ M6, W 108)

Quoted by al-Khargushi, the hadith scholar Ibn Jahdam al-Hamadani (d. 1023), al-Sarraj, al-Yafi`i, al-Sha`rani, and the great Damascene historian and theologian al-Dhahabi (d. 1348). Sarraj compares the union of lovers in this poem with Majnun's complete identification with Layla.

102. My Unique One

khaṣṣanī wāḥidī . . . ṭarqu (Shaybi[2] 310, Massignon[1] M39, Shaybi[1] 242)

Quoted by Sarraj, Ansari, and Ruzbihan Baqli.

This poem, which has a weak textual trail, is contested. Though accepted by Massignon, and by Shaybi in his first edition, it is dropped thereafter by Shaybi and Wazin, though it is accepted by Ruspoli (*Le Message de Hallâj l'Expatrié*, p. 268, no. 50) and others. Sirjani (p. 359) attributes the poem to Abu al-Hadid al-Misri. The crucial second line is variously construed. Initially Massignon read it as "I am the Truth, and as the Truth gives to him whom He wishes clothing in His own essence, may our separation no longer exist!" This would provide an example of "the great Hallajian sentence, *anā al-ḥaqq*" (Massignon[1], p. 75), which is otherwise difficult to confirm as an actual formulation in Hallaj's writings. On second thought, in his revised edition Massignon read it, quite obscurely, as *anā ḥaqqun* instead of *anā al-ḥaqq*: "I am truth in potential, and the Truth in act is its own potential . . ." (Massignon[2], p. 165). At that point, he felt that the intrusion of the notorious phrase "I am the Truth" was the mistake of a copyist. His last reflection was to read the phrase in question as *huwa ḥaqqun*: "He is the Truth, God is for God the Truth / who clothes (creation) with a garment (of glory), and this (glorious) garment of realities is, also, Truth!" (*Passion*, 3:63, following the conservative reading of 'Abd Allah al-Ansari, *Ṭabaqat al-sufiyya*, ed. 'Abd al-Hayy Habibi and Husayn Ahi [Tehran: Furughi, 2001], p. 316). My translation follows Shaybi. The key term "clothing" (*lābis*) probably has a negative sense of "concealing" here.

Verse 1. "chose" me (*khaṣṣanī*): "Unite me!" (*waḥḥidnī*, M39), "united me" (*waḥḥadanī*, *Passion*, 3:63). Massignon argued that *khaṣṣanī* "miserably weakens the thought," although it fits the meter better.

Verse 2. "I am the Truth, a truth that Truth deserved" (*anā al-ḥaqqu ḥuqqa lil-ḥaqqi ḥaqqun*) plays on four variations of the word *ḥaqq* ("truth," one of the ninety-nine names of God).

103. Your Place in My Heart

makānuka min qalbī . . . mawḍi'u (Shaybi[2] 299, Massignon[1] M35, W 138)

Quoted by Sarraj and Ruzbihan.

Massignon[F] (pp. 92, 148) adds a third verse in his translation, evidently based on Abu Hayyan al-Tawhidi's *al-Isharat al-ilahiyya* from a manuscript in Damascus (from the Zahiriyya library, fol. 110b), though the Arabic text does not appear in his edition or any other. It may be translated from the French as follows: "When I try to hide my soul, my conscience shows itself by the tears I shed."

104. Your Spirit Was Mixed

muzijat rūḥuka . . . al-zulāli (Shaybi[2] 326, Massignon[1] M47, W 150)

Transmitted by al-Khatib al-Baghdadi, al-Watwat, Ibn Kathir, al-Dhahabi, Ibn al-Dabbagh, and Ibn Abi al-Hadid.

105. I Have Pretended Patience

qad taṣabbartu . . . fu'ādī (Shaybi[2] 230, Massignon[1] M15, W 118)

Quoted by Ibn ʿArabi (who regards this verse as an example of pardonable intoxication) and Ibn al-Dabbagh.

Massignon[F] (p. 73) treats this poem, on the basis of rhyme, as the first half of a longer poem, with the second half being poem 16.

106. Glory to the One

subḥāna man aẓhara . . . al-thāqibi (Shaybi[2] 187, Massignon[1] M5, W 107)

Quoted by al-Khatib al-Baghdadi, al-Dhahabi, al-Daylami, Ruzbihan, Ibn Taymiyya, al-Qaysari, Ibn ʿAjiba, Ibn al-Jawzi, and Ibn Kathir.

Massignon sees here (verse 1) an allusion to God's creation of Adam and the display of divine qualities through him, to which the angels bowed down. Ruspoli (*Le Message de Hallâj l'Expatrié*, pp. 277–82) makes an extended comment on the evocation of Christian themes in this poem, particularly in the near-incarnationism of verse 2. While Ibn al-Khafif, the early Sufi of Shiraz, rejected this poem utterly, Ruzbihan was careful to explain that the Sufi teaching of Adamic manifestation of divine qualities is "clothing with divinity," not incarnation.

Verse 1. "whose humanity displayed" (*nāsūtuhu*): "who displayed his humanity" (*nāsūtahu*), Ruzbihan.

"secret" (*sirr*): "veil" (*sitr*), Daylami.

Verse 2. "to his creation" (*fi khalqihi*): "in creation" (*fil-khilqati*), Ruzbihan; "for his creation" (*li-khalqihi*), Qaysari; "veiled" (*muḥtajaban*), Watwat.

107. I Am the One That I Desire

anā man ahwā . . . badana (Shaybi[2] 342, Massignon[1] M57, W 161)

Quoted by Kalabadhi, Ghazali, Ruzbihan's Qur'an commentary (on Qur'an 6:59), Ibn ʿArabi, Qazwini, and others.

Shaybi acknowledges three additional verses as part of the same composition, though Massignon considers them additions from the following century:

> I am the one that I desire, the one I desire is I;
>   we are two spirits dwelling in a single body.
> When we were in the bond of desire,
>   proverbs were coined about us among the people.
> So when you have seen me, you have seen him,
>   and when you have seen him, you have seen us.
> You who ask questions about our story,
>   if you've seen us, you haven't divided us.
> His spirit is my spirit, my spirit is his spirit;
>   who has seen a spirit dwelling in two bodies?

108. You Are Flowing

anta bayn al-shaghafi . . . ajfāni (Shaybi[2] 355, Massignon[1] M61, W 165)

Transmitted by Sulami, ʿAbd Allah al-Ansari, Jami, and Abu Talib al-Makki.

109. I Entered into Creation

dakhaltu bi-nāsūtī . . . al-ṣidq (Shaybi² 313, Massignon¹ M42, W 145)

Verse 1. "creation" (*al-khalq*): two manuscripts read "the Truth" (*al-ḥaqq*).

"if it weren't for you, my divinity": Massignon translates, "If you were not my divinity."

"I would have fled sincerity" (*min al-sidq*): Wazin reads, "I would have departed with sincerity" (*fil-sidq*), but without any warrant for the emendation.

Verse 3. "youths" (*fitya*): "temptation" (*fitna*), *Akhbar* 53.

Ruspoli (*Le Message de Hallâj l'Expatrié*, p. 282, no. 62) suggests that "people" (*qawm*) means the saints, while "youths" evokes the Companions of the Cave (Qur'an, sura 18), identified with the Seven Sleepers of Ephesus.

Verse 4. "hearts" (*al-albāb*): "eyes" (*al-abṣār*), both times, in two manuscripts.

110. He Chose Me

huwa ijtabānī . . . sharrafanī (Shaybi² 304, Massignon¹ M60, W 164)

Found in the Geniza.

Verse 1. "he" (*huwa*), Wazin, Shaybi¹: "thus he" (*kādhā*), Massignon; "when he" (*lam-mā*), Shaybi².

"Honored me" (*sharrafanī*): "raised me up" (`arrajanī*), Massignon.

111. I Don't Play with Unity

lastu bil-tawḥīd . . . ashū (Shaybi² 390, Massignon¹ M67, W 171)

112. Hiding

mithāluka . . . tughību (Massignon¹ Y1, W 177)

113. Secret of My Secret

yā sirra sirrī . . . ḥayyi (Shaybi² 394, Massignon¹ M68, W 172)

Quoted by Ibn al-Qarih, Abu `Ali al-Farisi, al-Ma`arri, al-Muqaddisi, and Sarraj. Massignon has further comments in *Passion*, 3:47–48.

Verse 3. Massignon translates: "If I excuse myself before you, that would be (to argue) my ignorance (of your ubiquity), the (culpable) enormity of my doubt (of our union), of the excess of my stuttering (since you have taken me for a spokesman)."

114. Theory of Existence

lam yabqa baynī . . . tibyānī (Shaybi² 353, Massignon¹ Q8, W 92)

Quoted by Kalabadhi (whose verse 6 is accidentally omitted by Massignon), Suhrawardi, Qunawi, Ibn Jahdam, and Sha`rani. The order of verses here follows Kalabadhi (*Ta`arruf* 1536), which clarifies the structure. Although Shaybi considers it apocryphal, patently a product of Ibn `Arabi's school (presumably because of the term *wujūd*, translated here as "finding"), this poem is an artful defense of revelation against rationalism.

115. Concentration and Separation

al-jam`u afqadahum . . . bi-lā athari (Shaybi² 268, W 268)

Kalabadhi (*Ta`arruf* 1536–40) relates this verse anonymously in the midst of a particularly dense discussion of union and separation.

Verse 4. "time's condition" (*wal-ḥīnu ḥālun*), *Ta`arruf*: "the essence is a state" (*al-`ayn ḥālun*), Nuin/Janés

Verse 5. "when they were in his presence" (*minhu ḥīn al-waqt fī al-ḥaḍari*), *Ta`arruf*; "from sciences of time in presence" (*min `ulūm al-waqt fī al-ḥaḍari*), Shaybi.

116. How Will Union Take Place?

mawāṣilī . . . tajanni (Shaybi² 377, W 282)

Verse 7. "abandon me" (*ta`dunī*), Nuin/Janés; Wazin accepts Shaybi's reading "promise me" (*ta`idnī*) but suggests as an alternative "are singing" (*tughannī*).

117. Perfect Satisfaction

yā ḥabībī . . . fī makānī (Shaybi² 379, W 287)

Verse 2. "dazzling (*mubhir*), Nuin/Janés, following an alternative suggested by Shaybi, *bāhir*: "discerning" (*mubṣir*), Shaybi.

APPENDIX 1
ABBREVIATIONS

Note: All citations are by page number except as noted.

A Massignon's abbreviation for Hallajian poems actually by earlier authors

C Massignon's abbreviation for Hallajian poems actually by later authors

Essai Massignon, Louis. *Essai sur les origines du lexique technique de la mystique musulmane.* Nouvelle édition revue et considérablement augmentée. Paris: J. Vrin, 1968.

M Massignon's abbreviation for an occasional poem (*muqatta`a*)

Massignon[1] Massignon, Louis, ed. "Le *Dîwân* d'ál-Hallâj: Essai de reconstitution, édition, et traduction." *Journal Asiatique* (Janvier–Mars 1931): 1–158.

Massignon[2] Massignon, Louis. "Recherches nouvelles sur le «Diwan al-Hallaj» et sur ses sources." In *Mélanges Fuad Köprülü*, edited by Osman Turan, 159–72. Istanbul: Osman Yalçın, 1953.

Massignon[F] Hallâj, Husayn Mansûr. *Dîwân.* Translated by Louis Massignon. Documents Spirituels, 10. Paris: Éditions Cahiers du Sud, 1955. Reprint, Paris: Éditions du Seuil, 1981. Cited according to the 1981 edition.

Meier Meier, Fritz. "Ein wichtiger handschriftenfund zur sufik." *Oriens* 20 (1967): 60–106. English translation: "An Important Manuscript Find for Sufism," in *Essays on Islamic Piety and Mysticism*, translated by John O'Kane with Bernd Radtke, 135–88. Leiden: Brill, 1999. Cited by both the German and English pagination (e.g., 64/140 = German p. 64 / English p. 140).

MS, MSS manuscript, manuscripts

Passion Massignon, Louis. *The Passion of al-Hallaj, Mystic and Martyr of Islam.* Translated by Herbert Mason. 4 vols. Princeton, N.J.: Princeton University Press, 1982.

Q Massignon's abbreviation for a longer ode (*qasida*)

Shaybi[1] Shaybi, Kamil Mustafa al-, ed. *Sharh Diwan al-Hallaj Abi al-Mughith al-Husayn Ibn Mansur Ibn Mahma al-Baydawi, 244-309 H., 858-922 M.* Beirut: Maktabat al-Nahda, 1974. Reprint, Paris: Manshurat Asmar, 2005. Cited according to the 1974 edition.

Shaybi[2] Shaybi, Kamil Mustafa al-, ed. *Sharḥ Dīwān al-Ḥallāj, Abī al-Mughīth al-Ḥusayn ibn Manṣūr ibn Maḥmá al-Bayḍāwī, 244-309 H, 858-922 M: ma`a matn m.uḥaqqaq muḥarrar wa-tanṣīṣāt wa-muqaddima wa-fahāris.* 2nd ed., Cologne: Manshurat al-Jamal, 2007; reprint ed., 2012. Cited according to the 2007 edition.

Shaybi[3] *Diwan al-Hallaj Abi al-Mughith al-Husayn Ibn Mansur Ibn Mahma al-Baydawi*, ed. Kamil Mustafa al-Shaybi, wa yalayhi *Kitab al-Tawasin*, ed. Paul Nwiya. 3rd ed., Cologne: Manshurat al-Jamal, 1997; reprint ed., 2007. Cited according to the 1997 edition.

Sirjani   Sirjani, 'Ali ibn al-Hasan. *Sufism, Black and White: A Critical Edition of Kitab al-Bayad wa-l-Sawad of Abu l-Hasan al-Sirjani (d. ca. 470/1077).* Edited by Bilal Orfali and Nada Saab. Leiden: Brill, 2012.

Ta`arruf*   Mustamli Bukhari, Abu Ibrahim Isma'il ibn Muhammad. *Sharh al-ta`arruf li-madhhab al-tasawwuf. Edited by Muhammad Rawshan. 5 vols. Tehran: Intisharat-i Asatir, 1362–66/1984–88. This Persian commentary on the Arabic text of Muhammad al-Kalabadhi's *Kitab al-ta`arruf li-madhhab al-tasawwuf* is the preferred reference for this translation, because of its sound text edition and the often helpful commentary.

W   Wazin, `Abduh, ed. *Diwan al-Hallaj.* Bayrut: Dar al-Jadid, 1998.

Y   Massignon's abbreviation for a single-verse poem (*yatima*)

APPENDIX 2
THE LOST WORKS OF HALLAJ

The tenth-century bookseller Abu al-Faraj Muhammad al-Nadim (d. 990; often erroneously called Ibn al-Nadim) describes in his comprehensive *Index* (*al-Fihrist*) all the books available in Baghdad at the time. Of the forty-six titles he mentions as being the literary creations of Hallaj (listed below in translation), only the first (corresponding to the *Kitab al-Tawasin*) appears to relate to an actual surviving work by Hallaj, although the mention of his interpretations of Qur'anic verses may be connected to the scattered quotations from Hallaj that are found in the Qur'an commentaries of Sulami, Qushayri, and Rubihan Baqli. Thus the majority of the known writings of Hallaj may be assumed to be lost.

1. The Book of Ta' Sin [TS] of Eternity, the Greatest Jewel, and the Light-Giving Olive Tree
2. The Book of Temporal and Eternal Letters and the Universal Names
3. The Book of the Shade Extended, the Water Poured Forth, and the Eternal Life
4. The Book of the Conception of Light, Life, and Spirit
5. The Book of the Cabinet [of the Destruction of Eras]
6. The Book of Commentary on "Say, He God is One" [Qur. 112:1]
7. The Book of the Continuing in Eternity and the Eternally Continued
8. The Book of Recital of the Qur'an and the Furqan
9. The Book of the Creation of Humanity and the Exposition
10. The Book of the Cunning of Satan and the Command of the Sultan
11. The Book of the Roots and Branches
12. The Book of the Secret of the World and the Resurrected
13. The Book of Justice and Oneness
14. The Book of Politics, Caliphs, and Governors
15. The Book of Knowledge of Eternity and Annihilation
16. The Book of the Form of Things That Overshadow
17. The Book of the Light of the Light
18. The Book of Manifestations
19. The Book of Temples, the World, and the One Who Knows
20. The Book of Praise of the Prophet and "the Highest Likeness" [Qur. 16:60, 30:27]
21. The Book of the Strange and the Clear
22. The Book of the Point and the Beginning of Creation
23. The Book of the Resurrection and the Resurrections

24. The Book of Greatness and Majesty
25. The Book of Prayer and Divine Blessings
26. The Book of Treasures of Good Things, Known as the Separate Alif and the Composite Alif
27. The Book of the Ecstasies of Those with Knowledge
28. The Book of the Nature of Aspects of the Qur'an and the Admonition
29. The Book of Sincerity and Pure Intention
30. The Book of Examples and Topics
31. The Book of Certainty
32. The Book of Oneness
33. The Book of "The Star When It Sets" [Qur. 53]
34. The Book of "The Scattering Broadcast" [Qur. 51]
35. The Book of "He who enjoined upon you the Qur'an will return you to the place of returning" [Qur. 28:85]
36. The Book of the Pearl, addressed to Nasr al-Qushuri
37. The Book of Government, addressed to al-Husayn ibn Hamdan
38. The Book of "He Is He"
39. The Book of How He Was and How He Will Be
40. The Book of the First Existence
41. The Book of the Red Sulphur
42. The Book of al-Samari and His Answer
43. The Book of the Second Existence
44. The Book of "Without How"
45. The Book of Quality and Reality
46. The Book of Quality by Metaphor

Source: al-Husayn ibn Mansur Hallaj, *Diwan al-Hallaj: wa-yalihi akhbaruhu wa-tawasinuh*, ed. Sa`di Dannawi, 2nd ed. (Beirut: Dar Sadir, 2003), 19–21.

APPENDIX 3
STAGING THE POETRY: TWENTY-TWO SELECTIONS
FROM *NEWS OF HALLAJ (AKHBAR AL-HALLAJ)*
ILLUSTRATING HIS POEMS

Source: *Akhbar al-Ḥallaj. Recueil d'oraisons et d'exhortations du martyr mystique de l'Islam, Husayn Ibn Mansur Hallaj.* Edited by Louis Massignon and Paul Kraus. 3rd ed. Paris: J. Vrin, 1957. Translations by Carl W. Ernst.

Akhbar 2. It is related from the Chief Judge Abu Bakr ibn al-Haddad that he said, "On the night before the morning when al-Hallaj was killed, he stood and faced the direction of prayer, wearing his robe. He raised his hands and spoke many words that escaped recollection. But from what I recall of it, he said, 'We your witnesses [*shawahid*] take refuge in the glory of your might, and we seek illumination, so you may reveal what you wish of your character. For you are the one whose throne is in heaven, and you are "the one who is God in heaven, and God on earth" [Qur. 43:84]. It is you who manifest as you wish the likeness of your manifestation by your will, as "the most beautiful form" [i.e., Adam], the form in which the rational spirit exists by science and explanation, power and proof. You have inspired your witness [*shahid*, i.e., Hallaj], whose quality is "I am," with your essence, of which the quality is "He is." What of you, then, when you have likened yourself to my essence, at the end of my transformations, and you have called to my essence by my essence? You have shown the realities of my sciences and my miracles, by rising in my ascents to the celestial canopies of my eternities, in speech from my creatures. I have been seized, imprisoned, summoned, crucified, killed, and burned, and the stifling winds have collected my fragments. For that particle of burning sandalwood, the place where the temple of my manifestations is found, is larger than mountains!' Then he recited,

[78. Song of Death]

I cry to you the death of souls whose witness went astray;
    in what is beyond "how," one meets eternity's witness.
I cry to you the death of hearts, as long as clouds
    of revelation pour down seas of wisdom upon them.
I cry to you the death of truth's language, for long ago
    it died, and its imagined memory is like nothing.
I cry to you the death of rhetoric, and the surrender
    of every orator's words, in speech of understanding.
I cry to you the death of all thinkers' allusions;
    nothing remains of them but the erasing of their bones.
I cry the death, by your love! of the ethics of a people
    whose steeds were just the sorrow of repression.

All of them are gone; neither essence nor trace remains,
    like the passing of `Ad and the destruction of Iram.
They follow the crowd, imitating their fashion,
    dumber than cattle, and dumber than a beast of burden."[1]

Akhbar 10. From Abu al-Hasan `Ali ibn Ahmad ibn Mardawayh, who said, "I saw al-Hallaj in the Qati`a market in Baghdad, weeping and crying out three times, 'People! Hide me from God! For he has seized me, and he won't let me go, and I can't handle his presence! But I fear separation, lest I should be hidden and excluded. And woe to one who is hidden after being present, and is separated after union!' And the people wept with his weeping, until he reached the `Attab mosque, and he stopped at the door and began speaking words, some of which the people understood and some they did not.

"Some of what the people understood was that he said, 'People! He speaks to creatures from grace and manifests to them, then he conceals himself from them to educate them. For if he did not manifest himself, they would all be infidels. And if he did not conceal himself, they would all be deceived. And neither of the two states is permanent for them. But he has not been concealed from me for an instant, and I enjoy it until my humanity is destroyed in his divinity, and my body is made nothing by the lights of his essence. For I have no essence or trace, no face and no knowledge.'

"Some of what the people did not understand was that he said, 'Know that the temples are based on "Oh He," and bodies are moved by "Oh S [*ya sin*]." And "He" and "S" are two paths to the original dot.'[2]

"Then he recited,

[52. Illumination]

The covenant of prophecy is a lamp of light
    hung by revelation in the chamber of the heart.
By God, he blows the spirit's breath into my mind,
    into my thought—the breath of Israfil's last trumpet!
When he appeared to my spirit, to speak with me,
    I saw, in my rapture, Moses stand on Sinai."

Akhbar 11. `Abd al-Karim ibn `Abd al-Wahid al-Za`farani said,
    "I entered upon al-Hallaj while he was in the mosque, and around him was a crowd, and he was speaking. And the first thing that reached me of his speech was that he said, 'If an atom of what is in my heart encountered the mountains of the earth, they would melt; and if on the day of resurrection I was in the fire of hell, I would burn up the fire; and if I entered paradise, I would destroy its foundation.' Then he recited,

[51. Cramped]

I wonder at my all, how it bears a part of me,
    when just from the weight of a part, my earth can't bear me.
If there were a resting place on the breadth of earth,
    my heart would still be cramped by the breadth of creation."

Akhbar 12. Ahmad ibn Abi al-Fath ibn `Asim al-Baydawi said, "I heard al-Hallaj dictating to his students, 'God (Blessed be he who is transcendent, to whom praise belongs) is a single essence sustained by himself, isolated from any other by his eternity, united to his lordship apart from anything different. Nothing mingles with him, nor does any other mix with him. No place contains him, and no time comprehends him. Thought is not capable of him, and reflection does not conceive of him. Vision does not comprehend him, nor does weakness affect him.' Then his mood became tearful, and he recited:

[21. Transcendence]

My denial sanctifies you;
  my thought of you is confusing.
A love has astonished me,
  and a glance that's arched.
And the proof of love has shown
  that nearness is a deception.

"Then he said, 'My son, preserve your heart from the thought of him, and your tongue from mentioning him, and occupy them instead with continual gratitude toward him. For thinking about his essence, reflecting on his attributes, and speaking about his proof is a great sin and tremendous arrogance.'"

Akhbar 16. From Abu al-Hasan al-Halwani, who said, "I was present with al-Hallaj on the day of his execution, and they brought him bound in chains. He was swaggering in his chains, and laughing, and he recited,

[43. My Drinking Buddy]

My drinking buddy's not accused
  of anything unjust.
He pours for me the stuff he drinks,
  in the way of host and guest.
But then he called for the sword and mat
  when the cup had circled past.
So fares the drinker of pure wine,
  while summer's dog days last."

Akhbar 33. He said, "The essence of unity is contained in the conscience, the conscience is contained between two thoughts, and the thoughts are contained between two reflections; but reflection is swifter than the glances of the eye." Then he recited,

[56. Reason's Ears and Eyes]

For the lights of the light of lights, there are lights in creation,
  and for the secret, in the secret of the secret ones, there are secrets.
For existence in existents, there is a Giver of existence,
  who is fond of my heart, and he guides and chooses.
Consider with your reason's eye what I describe—
  for reason, there are watchful ears and eyes.

Akhbar 36. Ahmad ibn Faris said, "I saw al-Hallaj in the Qati`a market, standing at the door of the mosque and saying, 'People! When the Truth takes possession of a heart, He empties it of any other. When He sticks to someone, He annihilates him from anyone else. When He loves a devotee, he provokes His other devotees with enmity against him, so that the devotee approaches completely focused on Him. So what of me, when I can't find even a scent of God, nor any nearness to him for a second, and the people keep turning to me?' Then he wept, until the people of the market began to weep. And when they wept, he started laughing again until he nearly guffawed. Then he began to shout a series of agitated cries, and he recited,

[58. Ecstasies and States]

God makes all the ecstasies of Truth's ecstatic states,
    though great intellects fall short of these.
And ecstasy is nothing but a thought, and then a glance,
    drunk in flames beneath these consciences.
When God lives in one's conscience, it replicates
    three of the soul's states for the insightful:
One state destroys the conscience from the depth of its description
    but brings it back in ecstasy, in the state of one amazed.
A second state restrains conscience's heights, and faces
    a view erasing it from every viewer. . . ."

Akhbar 38. Ahmad ibn Qasim the ascetic said, "I heard al-Hallaj in the market of Baghdad shouting, 'People of Islam, save me! He does not release me and my soul so I can delight in it, and He does not seize me from my soul so I can be saved from it, and this is a teasing that I cannot endure.' Then he recited,

[18. The Soul's Punishment in the Body's Prison]

I've gathered, with my all, all of your all, my holy one.
    You strip away the veil from me as though you were inside me.
I turn my heart to things that are not you, but I only see
    my desolation is from that; in it you are my solace.
So that's why I'm in life's prison, removed
    from affection; so free me from this prison to you!"[3]

Akhbar 39. Abu al-Qasim `Abd Allah ibn Ja`far the Lover said, "When al-Hallaj entered Baghdad and his people gathered around him, one of the shaykhs was present with one of the rulers of Baghdad, called Abu Tahir al-Sawi, who loved the Sufis [*al-fuqara'*]. The shaykh asked him to invite people to a party, including al-Hallaj. A group of shaykhs responded to that, in his house, and al-Hallaj was present. And [the host] said to the singer, 'Recite what the shaykh chooses!' And by that he meant al-Hallaj. So al-Hallaj said, 'Only the sleeper is wakened, but the singer of the Sufis is not asleep!' Then the singer recited, and all were happy. Then al-Hallaj jumped into their midst and went into ecstasy, with the lights of reality radiating from him, reciting,

[81. Three Letters without Dots]

Three letters without dots
    then two dotted, and the speech is done.
One dotted letter resembles his ecstatic lovers,
    and everyone affirms the one that's left.
The other letters are a ciphered riddle,
    for there is no travel here, nor any station."[4]

Akhbar 40. It is also related of him that a man named Ibn Harun al-Mada'ini sought to join al-Hallaj and a group of the shaykhs of Baghdad, so they could debate with him. But when they gathered, Hallaj perceived ignorance in them, and he recited,

[82. You Who Are Unaware]

You who are unaware in ignorance of my rank,
    do you know nothing of my reality and my story?

For my worship of God is six letters,
    among which there are two with dots [N, Y].
Two are consonants: one a root [M], another [S] with its vowel
    in spelling related to "my faith" [imani].
And if the chief of letters [A] appears before them,
    a letter standing in the place of the second letter,
you'll view me standing in the place of Moses,
    in the light above Sinai when you see me.[5]

The people were astounded. Now Ibn Harun had a son who was in the throes of death, and he said to Hallaj, "Pray for him." And Hallaj said, "He is healed, so don't worry." And the son entered, as though he had never been sick. Everyone present marveled at that. Then Ibn Harun brought a sealed purse and said, "Shaykh, in this are three thousand dinars; spend them as you wish." The group was in a room overlooking the riverbank, and Hallaj took the purse and threw it in the Tigris, saying to the shaykhs, "Do you want to debate with me? What shall I debate? I know you are with the Truth, while I am with the false!" And he left. So the next day, Ibn Harun called the group and placed the purse before them, saying, "Yesterday I was thinking about what I gave to Hallaj, and then I regretted that. But then an hour did not go by when a Sufi, one of Hallaj's friends, came and said, 'The Shaykh sends you greetings, and says, "Don't have any regrets; here is your purse, for earth and sea obey the one who obeys God."'"

Akhbar 43. From Ibrahim ibn Fatik, who said, "I intruded upon al-Hallaj one night while he was in prayer, beginning to recite Sura 2 [The Cow]. He prayed a couple of cycles, until I fell asleep. When I awoke, I heard him reciting Sura 42 [Counsel], and I realized that he wanted to recite the complete text of the Qur'an. He completed the recitation in a single cycle, and in the second cycle he recited something and laughed at me, saying, 'Don't you see that I pray to please him? But whoever thinks that he has pleased him with devotion puts a price on his pleasure.' Then he laughed and recited,

[19. Lovers' Perfection]

When a youth reaches perfection from desire,
    and loses the remembered one in memory's pride,
he witnesses truth when desire attests to him
    that lovers' perfection is infidelity."

Akhbar 45. It is related from ʿAbd Allah ibn Tahir al-Azdi that he said, "I was quarreling with a Jew in the Baghdad market, and I happened to say to him, 'You dog!' And al-Husayn ibn Mansur [Hallaj] passed by and gazed upon me askance, and he said to me, 'Don't bark at your dog,' and quickly walked away. And when I finished with the argument, I sought him out, and I approached him, but he turned his face away from me. So I apologized to him, and he accepted that, and said, 'My son, all religions belong to God, who is great and mighty, and he occupies a community with each religion, not as their own choice, but as chosen for them. And one who blames another for the falsity of what is imposed upon him has decreed that he has chosen that for himself. But that is the teaching of the voluntarists [the Qadariyya], and [as the Prophet said,] "The Qadariyya are the dualists of this congregation." You should know that Judaism, Christianity, Islam, and other religions are diverse terms and different names, but their goal does not change or differ.' Then he recited these verses:

[63. I've Thought about Religions]

I've thought about religions as a thorough investigator,
 and I've found them to be a root with many branches.
So don't demand that a man have one religion, since
 he'll be turned away from the firm root. It's just
the root that should seek him, to explain to him
 all sublimities and meanings; then he'll understand."

Akhbar 46. It is related from Ibrahim ibn Sam`an that he said, "I saw Hallaj in the Mansur mosque, and I had two dinars in my pants that I tied there for something other than obeying God. Then a questioner asked for something, and Husayn said, 'Ibrahim, give him what you tied in your pants.' I was surprised, but he said, 'Don't be surprised; giving them as charity is better than what you had planned.' Then I said, 'Shaykh, how do you know this?' He said, 'Any heart emptied of what is not God sees what is concealed in the hidden and what is contained in the secret.' And I said, 'Help me with a word.' He said, 'One who seeks God by the letters of *with* finds him, and one who seeks him between the letters of *where* loses him. For he is sanctified beyond conceptual difficulties and transcends the thoughts of the artful.' Then he recited,

[83. Return to God]

Return to God, for God is the goal,
 and when you've reached the end, there is no God but he.
For he is *with* the creatures to whom he belongs,
 in the letters of "*with*," which mean "to sanctify."
Its meaning is on the lips of one who unravels a knot
 from its spelling for people who only pronounce it.
If you doubt, think of the saying of your Master,
 so that he says, against your doubt, "This is he!"
By the first letter, he is shown in height and depth;
 by the last letter, he is shown both far and near."[6]

Akhbar 50. He said, "I saw Hallaj enter the Mansur mosque, and he said, 'People! Listen to a word from me.' And many people gathered around him, including some who loved him and others who denied him. And he said, 'You should know that God most high has sentenced me to death, so kill me!' And some of the people wept. Then I stepped forward from the crowd and said, 'Shaykh! How should we kill a man who prays, fasts, and recites the Qur'an?' He replied, 'Shaykh! The reason for sparing a life goes beyond prayer, fasting, and reciting the Qur'an. So kill me, and you will receive a reward, while I will be delivered.' And the people wept and departed, but I followed him to his home and said, 'Shaykh! What is the meaning of this?' He said, 'There is no task in the world more important for the Muslims than killing me.' And I said to him, 'How is the path to God most high?' He replied, 'The path is between two, but there is no other with God.' I said, 'Explain!' He said, 'One who does not understand our allusions will not be guided by our expressions.' Then he said,

[98. Is It You or I?]

Is it you or I? That would be two gods in me;
 far, far be it from you to assert duality!
The "he-ness" that is yours is in my nothingness forever;
 my "all" added to your "all" would be a double disguise.

But where is your essence, from my vantage point when I see you,
  since my essence has become plain in the place where I am not?
And where is your face? It is the object of my gaze,
  whether in my inmost heart or in the glance of my eye.
Between you and me there is an "I am" that battles me,
  so take away, by your grace, this "I am" from in between.

Akhbar 51. From al-Husayn ibn Hamdan, who said, "I approached Hallaj one day and said to him, 'I wish to seek God, so where should I seek him?' His cheeks flushed, and he said, 'God transcends place and space, and he is isolated from the moment and from time; he goes beyond the heart and the soul, and is concealed from unveiling and exposition. He is sanctified from the comprehension of eyes and from the grasp of imagination's fancy. He is isolated from creatures by eternity, as they are isolated from him by time. How is the path to be sought to the one who has this quality?' Then he wept and said,

[65. Near and Far]

I said, "Dear friends, it's the sun; its light
  is near!" But there is distance in its approach."

Akhbar 52. He also said, "I heard Husayn in the Baghdad market, saying,

[39. Testament]

Hey there! Inform my friends that I
  have gone to sea and my ship is wrecked!
My death will be in the faith of the cross,
  and I want neither Mecca nor Medina.

So I followed him, and when he entered his house, he recited, 'God is most great,' and he recited Sura 1 [The Opening], and Sura 26 [The Poets] up to Sura 30 [The Romans], and when he reached the verse, 'and those to whom knowledge and faith has been given say . . .' [Qur'an 30:56], he repeated it and wept.[7] And when he greeted me, I said, 'Shaykh! You spoke in the market the speech of heresy, but then you performed prayer here, so what do you mean?' He said, 'That this accursed one should be killed,' indicating himself. So I said, 'Is it permitted to incite the people to falsehood?' He said, 'No, but I incite them to the truth, because in my opinion the killing of this one is a duty, and if they are zealous for their religion, they will be rewarded.'"

Akhbar 53. And from him also, he said, "He commanded the witnessing of his uniqueness, and forbade the description of the depth of his he-ness. He prohibited hearts from diving into his quality, and struck thoughts dumb at the comprehension of his divinity. Nothing appears from him to creatures except revelation, and revelation contains both truth and falsehood. So glory be to him who is mighty, who manifests to someone without any cause, and conceals himself from someone without any reason." Then he wept and recited,

[109. I Entered into Creation]

I entered into creation with my humanity, for you;
  if it weren't for you, my divinity, I would have fled sincerity.
For the language of knowledge is for speech and guidance,
  but the language of the hidden goes beyond speech.
You showed yourself to a people, but hid from certain youths,
  for they stray and wander, so you vanished from creation.

So sometimes you rise for hearts in the west,
and then again for eyes you set in the east.

Akhbar 55. And he said, "I heard Husayn say, 'Whoever wishes to reach the goal should leave the world behind his back.' Then he recited,

[72. Beware Consolation]

Beware consolation, my soul!
For power is from denial and surrender.
Beware the dawning that appears from
the niche of unveiled manifestation.
A part of me is based on part of my part,
but all of me longs for all of my all."

Akhbar 62. From Ibrahim ibn Muhammad al-Nahrawani, who said, "I saw Hallaj in the mosque of Nahrawan, praying in the corner, and he completed reciting the Qur'an in two cycles of prayer. The next morning, I greeted him, and I said, 'Shaykh, help me with a word about God's unity.' He said, 'When the devotee proclaims the unity of his Lord most high, he is affirming himself, and whoever affirms himself has introduced hidden idolatry. Only God is the one who affirms his own unity on the tongue of whatever creature he wishes. And if he affirms his unity on my tongue, that is his affair. Otherwise, my brother, what have I to do with the divine unity?' Then he recited,

[77. Intellect's Advice]

One who seeks him asking intellect's advice—
God grants him an astonishment that he enjoys.
He has mixed his secrets with deception,
saying in his astonishment, "Does he exist?""

Akhbar 66. From Ahmad ibn `Ata' ibn Hashim al-Karkhi, who said, "I went out one night into the desert, and I saw Hallaj looking for me. I went toward him and said, 'Peace be upon you, Shaykh.' He said, 'This dog's belly is hungry, so bring me stuffed lamb and two white flatbreads, while I wait here.' So I went and obtained what he asked for. And he tied the dog by one of its feet, and placed the lamb and the flatbreads in front of it until it ate; then he released the dog and sent it away, saying to me, 'This is what my soul asked from me, for days, and I have resisted until it forced me out tonight to seek this, but God most high has given me victory over it.' And he became happy, and recited in his ecstasy,

[47. Infidel]

I rejected the religion of God; infidelity is my duty,
because it is detestable to Muslims.

Then he said to me, 'Go back and don't follow me, or you will get hurt.' "

Akhbar *2. Hallaj wrote to Abu al-`Abbas ibn `Ata' from prison: "I do not know what to say. If I mention your goodness, I do not reach its depth, and if I mention your oppression, I would not express the reality. The experiences of your nearness appeared to us and consumed us and distracted us from finding your love. Then it inclined and joined to what it had wasted and destroyed, and it prevented the finding of the food of destruction. And it is as though I were there with blazing lights and torn veils, and the concealed was apparent, while the apparent was concealed, while I know nothing, and the one who never ceases is without ceasing." Then he sealed the letter and addressed it with these words:

[29. Prison Letter]

My concern for him is passion for you—
    you, toward whom our allusions point!
We are two spirits joined by longing
    in what touches you, and in your presence.[8]

Akhbar *3. Hallaj wrote to Abu al-`Abbas ibn `Ata', "May God lengthen your life for me, and eliminate your death for me, according to the best of what flows from fate, and what news relates. Nevertheless, you have the passions of the secrets of your love in my heart, and the kinds of the treasuries of your affection, which no book interprets, and no account computes, and no blame negates. And in that, I say,

[101. I Wrote You]

I wrote you, but I didn't write you;
    I only wrote my spirit, without a letter.
That's because the spirit is not separated
    from its lovers by a closing word.
So every letter coming from and reaching you
    without reply is my reply."

Notes

1. *Akhbar al-Ḥallaj: Recueil d'oraisons et d'exhortations du martyr mystique de l'Islam, Husayn Ibn Mansur Hallaj*, ed. Louis Massignon and Paul Kraus, 3rd ed. (Paris: J. Vrin, 1957), 2, with attention to the corrections proposed by Massignon in *Passion*, 1:13–16, nos. 21–28.

2. Massignon maintains that these cryptic expressions relate to Isma`ili teachings regarding the "speaker" (*natiq*) and the "silent one" (*samit*).

3. *Akhbar al-Ḥallaj*, 38, where one manuscript adds that this remark was one of the reasons for Hallaj's execution.

4. For the explanation of this riddle (= *tawhid*, unity), see the note to poem 81 of this book.

5. For the explanation of this riddle (= *namusi, ana musa*), see the note to poem 82.

6. This passage is not translated literally. Its rather technical argument contrasts the Arabic letters *mim* and `*ayn*, which form the preposition *ma`a* ("with"), against the letters *alif* and *nun*, which when combined by the adjectival letter *ya'* form the interrogative *ayn* ("where"). The point is that "with" connects the soul to God, while "where" is skeptical and turns away from God.

7. In this verse, the faithful inform the guilty that the day of resurrection has arrived.

8. Massignon treats the letter as a prayer addressed to God, while the "him" mentioned in the verses is Hallaj's companion Ibn `Ata' (the nominal addressee of the letter).

APPENDIX 4

EDITIONS AND TRANSLATIONS OF THE *DIWAN AL-HALLAJ*

Massignon's Editions of the *Diwan al-Hallaj*

The reconstitution of Hallaj's poems is largely due to the efforts of Louis Massignon. In 1914, Massignon published what amounted to a preliminary edition of the poems of Hallaj; in this edition, these poems did not stand alone but were embedded in the narratives of *Akhbar al-Hallaj* (*News of Hallaj*), based on four manuscripts.[1] Massignon extracted Hallaj's poems from their surrounding narratives later, after having found two additional closely related manuscripts, making a total of six. Following a term occurring in one of these manuscripts, he referred to this collection of six as a "registry" (*taqyid*) of poems circulating in mystical circles. He further divided this collection into two parts: the early *Diwan* proper, and a separate group of narratives in which the poems were embedded; those narratives he called "visits" (*ziyarat*) since they typically took the form of visits to Hallaj by various individuals during his imprisonment. In 1931 Massignon published the Arabic text of these poems, plus a number of additional poems transmitted in other sources (described below), accompanied by notes and a French translation. Massignon considered this 1931 publication to be the true first edition of the poems of Hallaj.[2]

Massignon's description of the manuscripts forming the basis of his edition was laconic, to the degree that he omitted to specify clearly the details of the titles and contents of each manuscript. A later editor, Kamil Mustafa al-Shaybi, furnishes the following information about their titles, together with the abbreviations used by Massignon:

J. "Some allusions of Husayn ibn Mansur al-Hallaj, his words, and his poems" (Massignon collection, gift of Tahir Jazairli).

K. "A Book on the life of the Shaykh and martyr, Husayn ibn Mansur al-Hallaj, the stations of Hallaj and his speeches" (Kazan, Central Oriental Library, Misc. no. 68)

L. "Registry of Certain Wisdom Sayings and Poems" (British Library, Add. 9692)

S. "Biography of Husayn ibn Mansur al-Hallaj" (Istanbul, Suleimaniyye no. 1028, fols. 358b–365b).

T. "Biography of Husayn ibn Mansur al-Hallaj and something of his writing, and what happened to him with the Caliph, and the nature of his execution" (Cairo, Dar al-Kutub, Ahmad Taymur Pasha, no. 129)

Berl. "The Story of Husayn ibn Mansur al-Hallaj" (Berlin, Staatsbibliothek, no. 3492, Petermann II 553, fols. 41a–43a; Ahlwardt 1240)

The widely varying titles of these texts, and the different literary forms they promise, indicate how challenging it is to see a coherent, unitary poetic collection in the sources.

227

But, to return to "the early *Diwan*," Massignon describes its format as follows: "It is a collection of homogeneous accounts, giving, nearly every time, after a rhyming ecstatic prayer (*munajah*; sometimes replaced by a series of sentences in ordinary prose), a short piece of verse (*shi`r*), in the form of a mnemonic commentary to meditate on."[3]

Massignon speculated that these poems had been actually collected between 933 and 936, in the region of Baghdad, by someone very familiar with the teachings of Hallaj but not from his immediate circle. The most likely editor, according to Massignon, was Faris Dinawari (d. 953), a Baghdadian Sufi who took refuge in Iran and eventually died in Samarqand. Massignon justified this account in part by arguing that Faris preserved the most authentic interpretation of the technical language of Hallaj's mysticism. According to this hypothesis, this early *Diwan* would have been the source drawn on by twenty later authors who quote these verses. Massignon derived twenty-one poems from this source that he considered authentic, with two others open to discussion. Acknowledging the conjectural nature of his reconstruction, Massignon admitted that at least two key interpreters of Hallaj, Farid al-Din `Attar and Ruzbihan Baqli, seem not to have been acquainted with this particular transmission of the poems of Hallaj in the early *Diwan*.

The other poems, which are contained in the "visits" texts, are found in separate sections of four of the "registry" manuscripts, either at the end or the beginning, and also occur in two other sources: a collection from an Istanbul manuscript ("Some poems of al-Hallaj," Istanbul, Fatih Efendi no. 2650, Köprülü 1620), and writings found in the Cairo Geniza, the repository of medieval papers preserved in the storage room of an ancient synagogue. Massignon proposed that the original basis for these accounts was a group of stories about visits to Hallaj in prison by his companion Shibli; these stories included reports of short sentences by Hallaj with verse commentary. These stories were expanded by legends of other visitors, including some whose presence would have been physically impossible at that time. All of these tales contain poems attributed to Hallaj, "some authentic or worthy of being so, others of a truly miserable composition," according to Massignon.[4] From the "visits" texts, Massignon extracted a total of forty-six authentic poems and eighteen considered dubious. It is noteworthy that Massignon drew eleven of these "visits" texts from manuscripts in Hebrew script found in the Cairo Geniza, indicating a significant Jewish readership for these poems of Hallaj.[5]

Outside the "registry," consisting of the six known manuscripts of the early *Diwan* and the "visits" texts, Massignon found seven additional poems in the prose work of Hallaj known as the *Tawasin*. This work, he argued, was transmitted by a different individual, Abu Bakr al-Wasiti, a Sufi who had a rival interpretation of Hallaj that was in conflict with the views of Faris; that is why there are no overlapping poems between the "registry" and the *Tawasin*. That attribution, however, is contested by Laury Silvers, who argues that Massignon has confused al-Wasiti with a well-known disciple of Hallaj, Abu Bakr al-Rabi`i; her research suggests that the latter is very likely the real editor of the *Tawasin*.[6] Additionally, Massignon collected another dozen poems attributed to Hallaj in different Sufi texts. Finally, for various reasons, he rejected a total of thirty-two poems found in the "registry" manuscripts, many of which have nonetheless found acceptance among later editors.[7] Given these fragmentary origins, it would be an exaggeration to say that Hallaj's poems had actually constituted a coherent "collected works" along the lines of the *diwan*s of the famous Arab poets of the `Abbasid era. Indeed, Massignon definitely produced a true first edition that, in effect, for the first time in history constituted Hallaj as the author of a large collection of poems, the largest corpus of verse by a single author in early Sufism; the subtitle to the 1931 edition (dropped from the 1955 edition) actually announces that it was "An Effort at Reconstitution, Edition and Translation." This edition consists of eighty-seven authentic poems (eleven odes, sixty-nine shorter pieces, and seven single verses) plus fifty-five poems considered apocryphal or misattributed; the latter section is further divided into four sections denoting poems borrowed from earlier or later authors, anonymous pieces in the style of Hallaj, and poems by later authors on Hallaj.[8]

Massignon followed his first edition with a supplementary article in 1953, offering a number of relatively minor additions and corrections and three new poems;[9] a second edition was then constituted by simply adding this list of corrections to a reproduction of the first edition.[10] The rather stilted French translations that accompanied Massignon's first edition were succeeded by a smoother French version, published independently in 1955, that included only those poems considered to be authentic and incorporated the textual changes proposed in the supplementary article.[11] Massignon eventually decided on a total of ninety-three poems as authentically by Hallaj (ten odes, seventy-seven shorter pieces, six single verses, about 360 verses in all), but he also took note of fifty-one attributed poems.[12] The work of Massignon is fundamental to any study of the poetry of Hallaj, and all subsequent work takes this as the starting point, although it is admittedly idiosyncratic. The Arabic text of Massignon's first edition is easily available on the internet.[13]

Later Editions of the *Diwan al-Hallaj*

Unnoticed by many, the Swiss Orientalist Fritz Meier contributed an important German article in 1967, in which he describes a remarkable manuscript (known as the Zahabi codex) from a Sufi library in Shiraz that contains many treatises on Islamic mysticism. One section of this manuscript consists of a version of the "visits" texts concerning Hallaj, with a number of variant readings of known poems, plus nine poems attributed to Hallaj that are not previously known from other sources; Meier published these poems along with a German translation, and his article was subsequently published in English translation. This important discovery needs to be included in any new consideration of Hallaj's poetry, though it has so far escaped the attention of Arab critics.[14]

The next major contribution to the study of Hallaj's poetry came from an Iraqi scholar, Kamil Mustafa al-Shaybi (1927–2006), who obtained his Ph.D. under the tutelage of the British Orientalist A. J. Arberry in Cambridge.[15] He produced a comprehensive Arabic commentary on Hallaj's poems in 1974 (Shaybi[1]), in the process identifying another four authentic pieces but discounting some accepted by Massignon; in all, he viewed ninety-one as authentic and included another fifty as possibly worthy of interest.[16] The following year, Shaybi published an abridgment of the first edition, containing essentially the same poems without commentary; eliminating two duplications, he counted eighty-nine poems as authentic (366 verses) in this collection, along with the same fifty attributed poems (194 verses) as in the previous edition.[17] In this and later editions, Shaybi adopted the convention, familiar to European literatures but novel for Arabic, of providing a title for each poem by way of explanation. Then in 1984, Shaybi produced an updated edition of the text without commentary, adding thirteen poems from the "registry" that Massignon had rejected, plus seven authentic poems along with sixteen attributed ones, as well as offering corrections to the previous edition. In all, this edition consists of 109 authentic poems (498 verses) plus sixty-three attributed ones (234 verses).[18] Then, in another updated edition, published in Germany in 1997 (without any new preface), al-Shaybi added one additional poem to the second edition, for a total of 110 authentic poems, accompanied by sixty-three attributed ones.[19] Parallel with the stand-alone editions, Shaybi released a considerably expanded version of his commentary in 1994 (Shaybi[2]), with 111 poems considered authentic (totaling 503 verses) plus sixty-six attributed poems (242 lines).[20] This book (Shaybi[2]) is indispensable for the detailed study of the poetry of Hallaj, and in many cases it offers the preferred readings.

Other editions of the poems of Hallaj have continued to appear, mostly based on Massignon and Shaybi.[21] Some of these editions are eccentric. One such was produced in 2003 by Hashim ʿUthman, a prolific author who writes mostly on the politics of Syria, with an emphasis on Shiʿism and sectarianism. He attempts to rescue the poems of Hallaj (of which he presents 111) from deliberate corruption inflicted by opponents, and he uses late Sufi dictionaries to establish what he believes to be the verses' authentic meaning.[22] ʿUthman's dramatic style of presentation, accompanied by the use of multiple question marks for emphasis, assumes that variations between different transmissions of Hallaj's poetry indicate that "hidden hands" have corrupted it. He is particularly suspicious of the validity of the text of Hallaj's prose work, the *Tawasin*. This is a somewhat conspiratorial approach, and it is not clear how reliance on Sufi dictionaries solves the problems of textual authenticity that the editor suspects. Nevertheless, several of the recent editions record interesting comments and disagreements over the variant readings, and therefore they are worth taking into consideration when contemplating Hallaj's textual tradition as a whole. What is most striking is that so many scholars have turned to the text of Hallaj's poetry as a challenging project in recent years; a total of seven new editions of the Arabic text have been published since 1996.[23] Perhaps the most thoughtful and attractive edition of the Arabic poems of Hallaj was produced in 1998 by the prominent Lebanese poet and literary critic ʿAbduh Wazin, a cultural editor for the Arabic newspaper *al-Hayat*. His highly intelligent reading of these poems counts eighty-nine authentic poems (twelve qasidas, sixty-nine shorter poems, and eight isolated verses) and adds ninety other attributed pieces.[24] Shaybi's commentary along with Wazin's edition form the bases for my translations, although the notes take other readings into consideration.

Translations of the Poetry of Hallaj

French. After Massignon, other French translators have entered the fray. An Egyptian psychoanalyst and cultural commentator, Sami-Ali, produced in 1985 an attractive translation of forty-nine short poems by Hallaj, accompanied by the Arabic text (lightly altering Massignon's edition) in cursive calligraphy. Sami-Ali argues that Massignon had an "unfaithful and encumbered" style in translation, which retained only the content without the suggestive power of the Arabic original.[25] He describes his own approach to translation as follows:

> To translate the poetry of Hallaj is to render the unity of a thought that the Unique unifies. It renders it as temporal structure that objectifies each poem through a bodily rhythm, a breathing that is proper to it, and of which the rhyme and conventional meter are only apparent aspects. This demands for each poem a meditation by which one recreates the moment when multiple echoes melt into a single voice, and the reflections into a crystalline density. Each poem filters one light that it shines at the same

time as the others. Above all, one should follow literally the words that allusively indicate by adapting themselves to the vibrations of a thought totally extended towards the Unique. Translation, then, is equivalent to a transfiguration where form and content coincide in a rhythmic organization that privileges alliteration, and where, in becoming another, the text becomes itself. One follows in this way the approach of a thought that, in Hallaj, only exists by that which it makes exist, disappearing in that which it makes appear. Only the quest for exactitude, from one word to a word that goes beyond the opposition of the spirit and the letter, can provide this poetry of the Truth with a beauty that is a function of truth.[26]

Another comprehensive French translation was produced by Stéphane Ruspoli, with 114 poems, based on Wazin's edition, plus a commentary that reads Hallaj in Christian and Gnostic terms.[27] Likewise, Chawki Abdelamir and Philippe Delarbre have produced another French version, based on Shaybi.[28]

Persian. Selected poems of Hallaj have been translated into Persian by a specialist in philosophy, Bizhan Ilahi, and by the master of the Ni`matullahi Sufi order, Dr. Javad Nurbakhsh. Nurbakhsh extracted twenty-nine poems from various early sources, without reference to Massignon.[29] Qasim Mir Akhuri produced a complete Persian translation of 112 poems, based on Massignon, Shaybi, and Dannawi.[30] Another Persian translation, based on Massignon's French version, was published in a bilingual edition by Jalal Alavinia in 2009.[31]

Urdu. There is also a complete translation of the *Diwan al-Hallaj* into Urdu by Muzaffar Iqbal, a Pakistani scholar who is a prolific author in English and Urdu on scientific, religious, and literary topics. His 1996 translation, accompanied by the Arabic text and a lengthy introduction by Nomanul Haqq, pays attention to the editions of Massignon (1931) and al-Shaybi (1974), and for a second edition in 2000, he considers Sa`di Dannawi's 1998 Arabic edition. He also consults the translations of Arthur Wormhoudt and Massignon, as well as Herbert Mason's translations in the English version of *The Passion of Hallaj*. Iqbal makes the following remarks about his view of the poetry of Hallaj:

> The poetry of the *Diwan al-Hallaj*, which explains the spiritual states of his internal moods and stations, can only in part be understood as an utterly personal experience, and this experience in the depths of the spirit only can become apparent from the overflowing of divine love. This translation can in no way change the principle of his poetry. His poetry is a sorrowful, heated, and astonishing effusion of divine love.[32]

Iqbal's highly personal reading of Hallaj's poetry reflects his view of Hallaj.

Spanish. There are several Spanish versions that are secondary translations from the French of Massignon.[33] But there is an independent Spanish translation by the eminent Spanish poet Clara Janés in collaboration with Arabic scholar Milagros Nuin (the two have previously produced a Spanish translation of the Arabic poems of al-Mutanabbi). Based on Sa`di Dannawi's edition, this translation includes the Arabic text and some insightful readings of the poems.[34]

Italian. A well-known Italian Orientalist, Alberto Ventura, has translated Hallaj's poetry into Italian as an independent publication and also as part of an anthology of Hallaj's writings.[35]

German. In 1968 Annemarie Schimmel, the noted specialist in Sufi studies, published an anthology of German translations of texts by and about Hallaj, including thirty-nine poems.[36] She later issued an abridged version featuring about half the poems of the earlier publication.[37]

English. Surprisingly, only perhaps half of Hallaj's strikingly original Arabic verses have been made available in literary English translation. A number of scholars have produced versions of single poems in the course of a larger argument (Stefan Sperl, Th. Emil Homerin, Michael Sells), but some have tackled several at a time, including Arthur Wormhoudt (ten poems), D. P. Brewster (four), and M. M. Badawi (seven). Martin Lings translated twenty of Hallaj's poems into Victorian-style verse in his *Sufi Poems* (2004). Herbert Mason translated two dozen poems in the course of producing an English version of Massignon's *Passion of Hallaj*. The present volume is the first comprehensive scholarly presentation of these poems.

Notes

1. Louis Massignon, *Quatre textes inédits, relatives à la biographie d'al Ḥosayn-ibn Manṣour al-Ḥallāj* (Paris: Librairie Orientaliste Paul Geuthner, 1914), part IV; see also Husayn Mansûr Hallâj, *Dîwân*, trans. Louis Massignon, Documents Spirituels, 10 (Paris: Éditions Cahiers du Sud, 1955; reprint ed., Paris: Éditions du Seuil, 1981), 3, and Louis Massignon, *The Passion of al-Hallaj, Mystic and Martyr of Islam*, trans. Herbert Mason, 4 vols. (Princeton: Princeton University Press, 1982), 4:xvi.

2. Louis Massignon, "Le *Dîwân* d'ál-Hallâj: Essai de reconstitution, édition, et traduction," *Journal Asiatique* (Janvier-Mars 1931): 1–158, cited as Massignon[1]. This was Massignon's first edition of the *Diwan al-Hallaj*. The remarks that follow are based on the introduction, 1–9.

3. Massignon[1], 3.

4. Ibid., 7.

5. P. B. Fenton, "Les traces d'Al-Ḥallāǧ, martyr mystique de l'islam, dans la tradition juive," *Annales islamologiques* 35 (2001): 101–27, especially p. 106. The eleven poems in the most significant Geniza manuscript (T-S Ka10.1, of which the first seven are in Hebrew script and the remaining four in Arabic script) correspond to Massignon's edition, as follows: (1) M26, (2) M6, (3) Q1, (4) M37, (5) A8, (6) M23, (7) M60, (8) M40, (9) M17, (10) M48, (11) M25. Massignon mistakenly identified the items numbered 6 and 8 with number 7. Fenton identifies several other Hallajian poems quoted in other Geniza documents and by later Hebrew authors: D1 (p. 107), M10 (p. 108, p. 122), M52 (p. 117), C11 (p. 121), M57 (p. 121), Q9 (p. 121). While Fenton (p. 104) observes that two of these poems (M48, M60) only exist in Hebrew script, the discovery of an Arabic-script version of M48 in the Shiraz manuscript described by Meier (see appendix 4) leaves M60 as the only poem by Hallaj represented exclusively in Hebrew script.

6. Laury Silvers, *A Soaring Minaret: Abu Bakr al-Wasiti and the Rise of Baghdadi Sufism* (Albany: State University of New York Press, 2010), 12–13.

7. Massignon[1], Index I.b, 148–51, providing only the first lines of the thirty-two omitted "registry" poems, of which five are from the Kazan manuscript and the remaining twenty-seven are from the London manuscript. Also listed in this index of "pieces excluded here as suspect" are five poems quoted by Kalabadhi (nos. 39, 41, 43, 45 [55 is a misprint], and 50, reproduced in Massignon's *Essai sur les origines du lexique technique*

de la mystique musulmane, pp. 353–56) and six poems from an anonymous Shadhili treatise (*al-Qawl al-sadid*), all of which Massignon judges as apocryphal.

8. Massignon in this first edition (see index with first lines, pp. 152–56) uses the following symbols to designate his numbering of the poems: Q for the eleven longer odes (*qasida*), M for the sixty-nine occasional pieces or fragments (*muqatta`a*), Y for seven solitary lines (*yatima*), A for eighteen poems by earlier authors, B for five poems from later authors, C for twenty-one anonymous pieces in the style of Hallaj, and D for seven later poems on Hallaj. Thus Q1 is the first ode, M1 the first piece, etc.

9. Louis Massignon, "Recherches nouvelles sur le «*Diwan al-Hallaj*» et sur ses sources," *Mélanges Fuad Köprülü* (Istanbul: Osman Yalçın, 1953), 351–68. The new poems are numbered Q8b, M16b, and Y8.

10. *Le Dîwân d'ál-Hallâj*, ed. Louis Massignon (Paris: Librairie Orientaliste Paul Geuthner, 1955), reproducing the article "Recherches nouvelles" on pp. 159–72; this combined edition is cited in this appendix as Massignon².

11. Husayn Mansûr Hallâj, *Dîwân*, trans. Louis Massignon, Documents Spirituels, 10 (Paris: Éditions Cahiers du Sud, 1955; reprint ed., Paris: Éditions du Seuil, 1981), cited here as Massignonᶠ.

12. *Passion*, 3:279.

13. *Diwan al-Hallaj*, jam` al-mustashriq al-faransi Louis Massignon, http://www.scribd.com/doc/410304/- (accessed March 7, 2010); this online edition (lacking any notes or textual apparatus) is also available at http://www.adab.com/modules.php?name=Sh3er&doWhat=lsq&shid=141&start=0 (accessed March 7, 2010).

14. Fritz Meier, "Ein wichtiger handschriftenfund zur sufik," *Oriens* 20 (1967): 60–106, especially 62–68; Fritz Meier, "An Important Manuscript Find for Sufism," in *Essays on Islamic Piety and Mysticism*, trans. John O'Kane with Bernd Radtke (Leiden: Brill, 1999), 135–88, especially 137–44. The manuscript also contains a commentary on a famous poem of Hallaj ("Is It You or I?"), with some additional lines, though it uses a pseudonym to refer to Hallaj as "`Abd Allah the Master" (p. 77 German/151 English). The new poems found in this manuscript are numbers 11, 35, 36, 38, 50, 67, 68, 69, and 91 in this translation; the manuscript also contains versions of 59, 98, and 104.

15. Kamil Mustafa Shaybi's Cambridge dissertation on the relationship between Sufism and Shi`ism was subsequently published in Arabic translation and frequently reprinted. See Kamil Mustafa al-Shaybi, *al-Sila bayna al-tasawwuf wa-al-tashayyu`* (Baghdad: Matba`at al-Zuhura, 1963).

16. Kamil Mustafa al-Shaybi, *Sharh Diwan al-Hallaj Abi Al-Mughith al-Husayn Ibn Mansur Ibn Mahma al-Baydawi, 244-309 H., 858-922 M.* (Beirut: Maktabat al-Nahda, 1974; repr., Paris: Manshurat Asmar, 2005), cited here as Shaybi¹. Shaybi adds to Massignon's selection one new authentic poem (no. 67), adds to the attributed list four poems that Massignon had only cited as "excluded" (therefore Shaybi uses an asterisk to mark these "inauthentic" poems with a separate numbering, as nos. *7, *26, *33, *40), and includes seven additional attributed poems (nos. *8, *14, *23, *39, *41, *48, *49). In this edition (Shaybi¹), no. 7 (p. 146) is a duplicate of no. 86 (p. 312), and no. 25 (p. 192) is a duplicate of no. 33 (p. 209).

17. Kamil Mustafa al-Shaybi, ed., *Diwan al-Hallaj* (Baghdad: Wizarat al-I`lam, 1974). This abridged first edition and subsequent editions by al-Shaybi also contain a useful index of vocabulary.

18. *Diwan al-Hallaj Abi al-Mughith al-Husayn Ibn Mansur Ibn Mahma al-Baydawi*, ed. Kamil Mustafa al-Shaybi, 2nd. ed. (Baghdad: Dar Afaq `Arabiyya lil-Sihafa wal-Nashr,

1984). This edition draws on the thirty-two poems in the "registry" that Massignon had rejected to propose fifteen as authentic poems (in Shaybi's 1984 edition, nos. 24, 44, 45, 46, 59, 60, 65, 68, 72, 78, 93, 94, 95, 96, and 97) and thirteen as attributed poems (nos.*1, *2, *3, *11, *24, *25, *31, *40, *49, *50, *51, *57, and *58; again, Shaybi's 1984 edition uses asterisks to mark these poems as inauthentic, in a separate numbered series,). Shaybi restores as authentic poems five quoted by Kalabadhi that Massignon had rejected (nos. 41, 42, 43, 108, and 109). Shaybi does not include Massignon's M29 and Y1 at all, classifies Massignon's A1 as authentic (no. 98), and demotes Massignon's M23 to attributed status (no. *32). Shaybi does not indicate the sources for these new poems here, alluding instead in a vague fashion to "newly discovered manuscripts," though these poems may be identified from the opening lines (cited in Massignon[1], pp. 148–51), as coming from either the "registry" or Kalabadhi; in his second edition of the commentary, Shaybi[2] provides exact references for all these poems.

19. *Diwan al-Hallaj Abi Al-Mughith al-Husayn Ibn Mansur Ibn Mahma al-Baydawi*, ed. Kamil Mustafa al-Shaybi, wa yalihi *Kitab al-Tawasin*, ed. Paul Nwiya (3rd ed., Cologne: Manshurat al-Jamal, 1997; repr., 2007), cited here as Shaybi[3]. Here Shaybi restores one authentic poem from Massignon[2] (M16b) that that he and other editors had previously overlooked (Shaybi[3], no. 25).

20. Kamil Mustafa al-Shaybi, *Sharh diwan al-Hallaj* (2nd ed., Cologne: Manshurat al-Jamal, 2007; repr., 2012), cited here as Shaybi[2].

21. `Abd al-Ilah Nabhan and `Abd al-Latif Rawi, ed., *Turath al-Hallaj, akhbaruhu, diwanuhu, tawasinuhu*, Silsilah al-Turathiyah, vol. 3 (Hims: Dar al-Dhakira, 1996), offers brief annotations based on Shaybi's commentary. The edition of *Akhbar al-Hallaj* by `Abd al-Hafiz ibn Muhammad Madani Hashim (Cairo: Maktabat al-Jundi, n.d.), which might be supposed relevant to the *Diwan*, is an unacknowledged reproduction of the edition edited by Massignon and Kraus.

22. al-Husayn ibn Mansur Hallaj, *Diwan al-Hallaj*, ed. Hashim `Uthman (Beirut: Mu'assasat al-Nur lil-Matbu`at, 2003). `Uthman relies on the previous editions of Shaybi, al-Nabhan, and Qasim Muhammad `Abbas.

23. New editions include Sa`di Dannawi, ed., *Diwan al-Hallaj: Wa-yalihi Akhbaruhu wa-Tawasinuh* (Beirut: Dar Sadir, 1998; repr., Beirut: Dar Sadir, 2003); `Abd al-Nasir Abu Harun and Mahmud Fuad `Azzam, ed., *Diwan al-Hallaj* (Damascus: al-Hikma, 1998); Muhammad Basil `Uyun al-Sud, ed., *Diwan al-Hallaj: Wa-ma`ahu akhbar al-Hallaj wa-kitab al-tawasin*, 2nd ed. (Beirut: Dar al-Kutub al-`Ilmiyya, 2002); Qasim Muhammad `Abbas, *Al-Hallaj: Al-a`mal al-kamila* (Beirut: Riyad al-Rayyis lil-Kutub wa-al-Nashr, 2002).

24. al-Husayn ibn Mansur Hallaj, *Diwan al-Hallaj*, ed. `Abduh Wazin (Beirut: Dar al-Jadid, 1998). Wazin largely follows Shaybi[2], although he agrees with Massignon in promoting nine of eleven poems that Shaybi considers attributed (Shaybi[2], nos. *4, *9, *21, *29, *32, *33, *37, *38, *44, *45, and *46) to the status of authentic (Wazin, pp. 105, 109, 179, 134, 113, 140, 156, 154, and 88). He also demotes eleven of Shaybi's authentic poems (Shaybi[2], nos. 6, 8, 18, 27, 33, 39, 66, 84, 85, 86, and 105) to attributed status (Wazin, pp. 211, 214, 230, 189, 225, 193, 184, 209, 204, 200, and 205), and omits two more altogether (Shaybi[2], nos. *29 and *40). Moreover, Wazin takes all the new poems from the "registry" and Kalabadhi that Shaybi[2] proposes as authentic and places them in a separate appendix as doubtful (Wazin, pp. 265–90) under the mistaken impression that Shaybi does not indicate their sources.

25. Hussein Mansour Hallaj, *Poèmes Mystiques*, trans. Sami-Ali, La Bibliothèque de l'Islam (Paris: Sindbad, 1985), 21.

26. Ibid., 20.

27. Stéphane Ruspoli, trans., *Le message de Hallâj l'Expatrié: Recueil du Diwân, Hymnes et Prières, Sentences prophétiques et philosophiques* (Paris: Cerf, 2005).

28. Hussein Mansour al-Hallaj, *Dîwân*, trans. Chawki Abdelamir and Philippe Delarbre (Monaco: Éd. du Rocher, 2008).

29. Bizhan Ilahi, *Ash`ar-i Hallaj*, Intisharat-i Anjuman-i Shahanshahi-i Falsafa-i Iran, 2 (Tehran: Anjuman-i Shahanshahi Falsafa-i Iran, 1975); Javad Nurbakhsh, *Hallaj: Shahid-i `ishq-i ilahi* (Tehran: Javad Nurbakhsh, 1373/1995, with the Persian translations of Hallaj's poems on 169–84.

30. Qasim Mir Akhuri, *Divan-i Hallaj va guzari bar andisha va ta`birat-i `irfani* (Tehran: Qasida, 1999); reprinted in *Majmu`a-i Athar-i Hallaj: Tavasin, Kitab-i Rivayat, Tafsir-i Qur'an, Kitab-i Kalimat, Tajrubiyat-i `irfani va ash`ar* (Tehran: Nashr-i Yadavaran, 1379/2000; repr., Tehran: Intisharat-i Shafi`i, 2007), 368–428, citing the 1379/2000 edition.

31. Husayn Mansûr Hallâj, *Dîwân*, French trans. Louis Massignon, Persian trans. Jalal Alavinia (Paris: Lettres Persanes, 2009).

32. Mansur Hallaj, *Divan*, trans. Muzaffar Iqbal (Karachi: Daniyal, 1996; 2nd ed., 2000), 60, citing the 1996 edition.

33. Al-Hallaj, *Diwan*, trans. Leonor Calvera (Rosario: Ediciones del Peregrino, 1983; repr., Buenos Aires: Ediciones del Peregrino, 1984); al-Husayn ibn Mansur Hallaj, *Poemas De Amor Divino: Poemario Sufi*, trans. Francisco F. Villalba, Libros De Los Malos Tiempos, 13 (Madrid: Miraguano Ediciones, 1986); Soledad Fariña, "Poemas místicos de Hallaj," *Cyber Humanitatis* 28 (Spring 2003), accessed April 4, 2010, http://www.cyberhumanitatis.uchile.cl/index.php/RCH/article/view/5723/5591; al-Hallaj, *Diván*, trans. María Tabuyo and Agustín López, Los Pequeños Libros De La Sabiduría, 117 (Palma de Mallorca: José J. de Olañeta, 2005).

34. Al-Husayn b. Mansur al-Hallay, *Diván*, trans. Clara Janés and Milagros Nuin (Madrid: Ediciones del Oriente y del Mediterráneo, 2002). (Spanish Arabists transliterate the Arabic letter *jim* as "Y".)

35. *Diwan al-Hallaj*, trans. Alberto Ventura (Genoa: Marietti, 1987); *Al-Hallaj, Il Cristo del Islam: Scritti Mistici*, trans. Alberto Ventura (Milan: Mondadori, 2007).

36. Annemarie Schimmel, *Al-Halladsch, Märtyrer der Gottesliebe* (Köln: Hegner, 1968), 38–50.

37. Al-Halladsch, *"O Leute, Rettet Mich Vor Gott": Worte Verzehrender Gottessehnsucht*, trans. Annemarie Schimmel, Texte Zum Nachdenken, Bd. 47 (Freiburg im Breisgau: Herderbücherei, 1985; repr., 1995).

APPENDIX 5
HOW RUMI QUOTED HALLAJ

For many admirers of Sufism, the central figure is the great Persian poet Jalal al-Din Rumi (d. 1273). But before Rumi there was Hallaj. For Rumi, who lived in the thirteenth century, Hallaj was a figure from a long-ago foundational era, born well over three hundred years earlier. Like another great Persian poet by the name of Farid al-Din ʿAttar (who claimed to have received a spiritual initiation from Hallaj), Rumi was deeply familiar with the Arabic poetry of the Sufi martyr, whose fate he often recalled.[1] It is not surprising that the Persian Sufi poets were drawn to Hallaj's expressions of self-sacrifice, as found in poems like number 44, "Kill Me, Friends." Rumi was particularly fond of this poem, and he echoed it in his own Persian verse on a number of occasions, giving a remarkable bilingual character to his poetry (in the translations below, the Persian text is in a normal type font, while passages in Arabic are in bold). One of these examples is a powerful lyric with a driving rhythm (no. 386 of the *Divan-i Shams* in the standard numbering of Foruzanfar), much of which is devoted to the depiction of feminine angels. It concludes, however, with the invocation of silence before the indescribable experience of love:

> I went silent when I saw a speaker more fluent than me;
> I die in front of him and recite, "**Kill me, friends!**"
> When Shams-i Tabrizi opens his mouth like sugar,
> both bones and body are leaping from joy.[2]

It is striking that Rumi quotes this line in the context of unmatched eloquence. Rather than an embrace of martyrdom, the quotation from Hallaj is an ecstatic cry of recognition.

Another lyric poem of Rumi (no. 2086) quoting the same poem of Hallaj features a strong mournful pause in the midst of every line, lamenting the absence of the beloved. It is an unusually long Persian ghazal—twenty-four verses—containing a passage of ten verses that are all in Arabic, with the exception of a single verse in Turkish. Hallaj's poem, the first verse of the Arabic section, is introduced as follows:

> Strange! I'm telling the rest of the story again.
> No, I'm silent; you speak, sweet-voiced singer!
> "**Kill me, friends, for in my killing is my life,
> and life is in death**" in lovers' passions.[3]

Here too, Rumi quotes this famous line from Hallaj when reaching for an example of eloquent speech.

Rumi returns to this poem in a ghazal of fifteen verses (no. 2813) that is literally framed by quotations from Hallaj. It begins with the first verse of Hallaj's poem and follows with a similar Arabic half verse:

"Kill me, friends, for in my killing is my life,
   and my death is in my life and my life is in my death."
Kill me, for my body melts; the wine cup is my fate.
   Go, shatter the chains, my love, if you want salvation.[4]

The ghazal concludes with another evocation of intoxicating feminine spirits that segues into Hallaj again (no. 44, verse 19), inviting the reader to complete the rest of the poem:

From the cup of heroes you will reach the illustrated fancies,
   striding by the heart's path like guarded women,
"And running waitresses with running waters—"
   you tell the rest, for I'm drunk from these drinks![5]

Clearly this is a poem that Rumi expected everyone to know.

But "Kill Me, Friends" is not the only one of Hallaj's works that Rumi quotes. Here is a passage from the *Mathnawi* where Rumi starts by offering variations on Hallaj's "kill me, friends," the verse of martyrdom:

I was tested—my death is in my life;
   when I am freed from this life, there is eternity.
"Kill me, kill me, my dear friends;
   in my killing is a life, in my life!"
You bright face, you spirit of eternity!
   My spirit melts—renew me with your presence![6]

But then Rumi pivots to quote a line from a different poem by Hallaj (no. 6, "Alchemical Expressions"), which offers a twist on standard love poetry. It is a line that Rumi uses elsewhere (*Divan-i Shams*, no. 264) to introduce an artful bilingual poem of alternating Arabic and Persian lines.[7] Here he continues,

"I have a lover whose love is inside of me,
   and if he wants, he strolls across my face."
Speak Persian though Arabic be sweeter:
   love itself has a hundred other languages.
When the scent of that lover flies,
   all those languages are left astonished.[8]

Here, too, Hallaj is the standard of Arabic eloquence that, for Rumi, offers the closest possible approach to transcendence.

Notes

1. An overview of Rumi's references to Hallaj is provided by Muhammad Najari and Kamil Ahmadnazhad in "Hallaj dar athar-i Mawlana" [Hallaj in the writings of Rumi], *Fasl-nama-yi adabiyat-i `irfani wa ustura-shinakhti* [*Yearbook of Mystical Literature and Mythology*], vol. 9, no. 32)1392/2014(, 1–10.

2. Mawlavi [Rumi], *Divan-i Shams*, ghazal 386, verses 11–12, https://ganjoor.net /moulavi/shams/ghazalsh/sh386/.

3. Ibid., ghazal 2086, verses 14–15, https://ganjoor.net/moulavi/shams/ghazalsh /sh2086/.

4. Ibid., ghazal 2813, verses 1–2, https://ganjoor.net/moulavi/shams/ghazalsh /sh2813/.

5. Ibid., ghazal 2813, verses 14–15, https://ganjoor.net/moulavi/shams/ghazalsh /sh2813/.

6. Jalal al-Din Muhammad Balkhi [Rumi], *Mathnawi*, ed. Muhammad Isti`lami (Tehran: Zawwar, 1363/1984), 3:177, verses 3841–42.

7. Rumi, *Divan-i Shams*, ghazal 264, verses 1–7, https://ganjoor.net/moulavi/shams /ghazalsh/sh264/.

8. Ibid., verses 3843–45.

The index below provides references to the published editions of the original Arabic texts for each poem translated in this volume (citing the first line). Bibliographic details are provided in appendix 1, and the editions themselves are discussed in appendix 4. References are to page numbers except for Massignon[1], which is cited by the numbering of the poems. Under Massignon[1], "I.b." indicates that the text is from the six "registry" manuscripts, and "Kal" is short for Kalabadhi's *Kitab al-ta`arruf*. Massignon judges poems from these texts to be inauthentic, only publishing the first lines. Likewise, poems in Shaybi[2] with a page number above 402 or in Wazin with a number above 182 are considered inauthentic by those editors.

Poem No.	Massignon[1]	Shaybi[2]	Wazin	Meier
1	M8	202	110	
2	M3	403	105	
3	C12	165	224	
4	M10	216	112	
5	M23	453	126	
6	M32	290	135	
7	M9	197	111	
8	M31	459	134	
9	I.b.3	319	278	
10	I.b.20	320	279	
11				64/140
12	I.b.26	340	281	
13	I.b.1		284	
14	I.b.28		288	
15	M18	252	121	
16	M16	233	119	
17	M25	261	128	
18	M30	284	133	
19	M20	246	123	

Poem No.	Massignon[1]	Shaybi[2]	Wazin	Meier
20	M13	229	116	
21	M28–M29	279	132	
22	M11	214	114	
23	M26	263	129	
24	M34	297	137	
25	M24	259	127	
26	M52	484	156	
27	M43	397	146	
28	M62	370	166	
29	M44	392	147	
30	M64	372	168	
31	M54	340	158	
32	M59	373	163	
33	M16b	234		
34	Q9	350	94	
35				63/138
36				65/140
37	I.b.6	232	267	
38				65/140
39	M56	374	160	
40	M36	300	139	
41	M14	230	117	
42	Y7	474	183	
43	M37	466	140	
44	Q10	204	96	
45	M7	412	109	
46	M51	487	154	
47	Y2	225	178	
48	Y4	267	180	
49	Kal 1659	399	290	
50				64/139
51	M33	296	136	
52	M21	235	124	
53	M63	373	167	
54	M17	265	120	

Poem No.	Massignon[1]	Shaybi[2]	Wazin	Meier
55	M53	332	157	
56	M22	240	125	
57	Q11	254	98	
58	M19	249	122	
59	M48	328	151	66/142
60	M40	310	143	
61	M38	318	141	
62	M12	212	115	
63	M50	335	153	
64	M69	391	173	
65	Y3	435	179	
66	I.b.14	304	275	
67				65/141
68				64/139
69				63/138
70	Q8b	177	99	
71	M1	175	103	
72	M46	392	149	
73	M45	325	148	
74	M4	171	106	
75	Q1	182	79	
76	M2	168	104	
77	M66	388	170	
78	Q6	495	88	
79	I.b.13	305	276	
80	M27	263	130	
81	M49	334	152	
82	M58	358	162	
83	M65	386	168	
84	I.b.11	274	273	
85	Q4	277	84	
86	Q3	244	83	
87	Y5		181	
88	Q2	194	81	
89	Q7	337	90	

Poem No.	Massignon[1]	Shaybi[2]	Wazin	Meier
90	Q5	286	86	
91				66/141
92		398	289	
93	Kal 1458	271	269	
94	Kal 1498	272	270	
95	I.b.10	273	272	
96	I.b.22	331	280	
97	Y8			
98	M55	364	159	62/137
99	Y6	302	182	
100	M41	307	144	
101	M6	192	108	
102	M39	310	142	
103	M35	299	138	
104	M47	326	150	66/141
105	M15	230	118	
106	M5	187	107	
107	M57	342	161	
108	M61	354	165	
109	M42	313	145	
110	M60	304	164	
111	M67	390	171	
112	Y1		177	
113	M68	394	172	
114	Q8	353	92	
115	Kal 1536	268	268	
116		377	282	
117	I.b.30		287	

INDEX 2
ARABIC FIRST LINES OF POEMS

The original Arabic text of the poems translated in this book may be located in this table. It contains transliterations of the opening and closing words of the first line of each poem, arranged alphabetically by the starting words. The closing words indicate the end rhyme, the organizing feature of Arabic *diwan*s, to aid the reader in finding these poems in Arabic text editions. Numbers in the right-hand column indicate the numbering of the poem in this translation.

245

INDEX 3
CONCORDANCE OF TRANSLATED POEMS WITH EPISODES IN *AKHBAR AL-HALLAJ*

Note: Numbers of episodes from Akhbar al-Hallaj prefaced by an asterisk indicate a second set of texts that begins a new numbering sequence.

Poem No.	Akhbar al-Hallaj	Poem No.	Akhbar al-Hallaj
18	38	63	45
19	43	65	51
21	12	72	55
29	*2	77	62
39	52	78	2
43	16	81	39
47	66	82	40
51	11	83	46
52	10	98	50
56	33	101	*3
58	36	109	53

INDEX 4
CONCORDANCE OF TRANSLATED POEMS WITH MASSIGNON'S EDITION OF THE *DIWAN AL-HALLAJ*

Massignon[1]	Poem No.	Massignon[1]	Poem No.
Q1	75	M33	51
Q2	88	M34	24
Q3	86	M35	103
Q4	85	M36	40
Q5	90	M37	43
Q6	78	M38	61
Q7	89	M39	102
Q8	114	M40	60
Q8b	70	M41	100
Q9	34	M42	109
Q10	44	M43	27
Q11	57	M44	29
M1	71	M45	73
M2	76	M46	72
M3	2	M47	104
M4	74	M48	59
M5	106	M49	81
M6	101	M50	63
M7	45	M51	46
M8	1	M52	26
M9	7	M53	55
M10	4	M54	31
M11	22	M55	98
M12	62	M56	39
M13	20	M57	107

Massignon[1]	Poem No.	Massignon[1]	Poem No.
M14	41	M58	82
M15	105	M59	32
M16	16	M60	110
M16b	33	M61	108
M17	54	M62	28
M18	15	M63	53
M19	58	M64	30
M20	19	M65	83
M21	52	M66	77
M22	56	M67	111
M23	5	M68	113
M24	25	M69	64
M25	17	Y1	112
M26	23	Y2	47
M27	80	Y3	65
M28	21	Y4	48
M29	21	Y5	87
M30	18	Y6	99
M31	8	Y7	42
M32	6	Y8	97

The Qur'anic verses listed below are mentioned either in prefaces to translations (e.g., 4T = translation of poem 4) or in notes (88N = notes to poem 88).

Qur'an verse	Poem no.
2:154	70N
6:59	107N
7:12	20T
7:155	43N
10:35	54N
16:46	90N
16:47	90N
17:1	49N
18	109N
24:35	52T, 52N
24:43	59N
26:224–25	16T, 16N
28:30	43N
33:72	28T, 28N
35:27	88N
36:43	54N
37:89	10T
39:39	48N
42:17	43N
53:7	69T
53:16	59N
53:8	4T
109:6	8T, 8N